Book 1 of the Monumental Moments Series

Vessel of Noble Use

A Memoir by Christie Jones

To contact the author:

www.vesselofnobleuse.com

DEDICATION

I dedicate this book to You, my Lord and my King.
You truly are King of my heart.
You gave me life; I humbly give it back to you for Your service.
I deeply desire to be Your vessel of noble use for Your glory.
I'm nothing without You.
It's an honor to serve You, my Valiant Warrior King!

BUT IN A GREAT HOUSE THERE ARE
NOT ONLY VESSELS OF GOLD AND
SILVER, BUT ALSO UTENSILS OF WOOD
AND EARTHENWARE, AND SOME FOR
HONORABLE AND NOBLE USE AND SOME
FOR MENIAL AND IGNOBLE USE.

SO WHOEVER CLEANSES HIMSELF FROM
WHAT IS IGNOBLE AND UNCLEAN, WHO
SEPARATES HIMSELF FROM CONTACT
WITH CONTAMINATING AND CORRUPTING
INFLUENCES WILL THEN HIMSELF **BE A VESSEL
SET APART AND USEFUL FOR HONORABLE
AND NOBLE PURPOSES, CONSECRATED
AND PROFITABLE TO THE MASTER, FIT
AND READY FOR ANY GOOD WORK.**

—2 TIMOTHY 2:20-21, AMP

ACKNOWLEDGMENTS

I already thanked Papa, my Bestie Jesus, and Holy Spirit at the beginning of the book, it is dedicated to them to be used as they see fit.

Jonesie ... you held me close many times as I warriored through getting this book completed. Much of it is your story too. I love how you love me.

My beloved kiddos ... you have been supportive in your own ways and have been my biggest cheerleaders.

Wendy Walters ... Holy Spirit flows so beautifully in you and through you. The softness of your words brought out the best in me. You are more than my editor and publishing support, you are my treasured friend. I've had more laughter than tears throughout this process because of your style of mentoring and coaching.

Kate Walters ... you are wise beyond your years and truly a woman of excellence.

Bob and Polly Hamp ... Freedom training and learning under your God given anointing has directly impacted my journey into living life to the fullest with exuberance and peace.

Bill and Kathy Johnson ... you were the first to train me to see and hear God in different ways. Your LOVE has created a healthy atmosphere to break through into who I am today.

Gary and Linda Hall ... you saw something great in two young, inexperienced Christ followers. May the good Lord bless all that you touch. The two of you are a power couple that minister in your everyday lives. You change the atmosphere and influence change.

Them dang Joneses ... I married into this great family and I am blessed by each and every one of you. Some of you weren't even born yet in this book but will be known far and wide as the pages unfold in the future. I want the world to know how great you are. Thank you all for loving us through the good, the bad, the ugly and the really ugly times. Family is important!

Page Geske ... my book twin and author of your own story, *Milepost 95, From Wreckage to Redemption*. We birthed our books together after meeting at Wendy Walters' Release the Writer event. We haven't competed against each other because we understand that God is using each one of our stories to advance His Kingdom in His own way. I love you deeply. I am blessed to run alongside you in this marathon called LIFE.

Dr. Rachel Philip, Jim and Dottie Nation and Suzie Fuller, you all believed in me and trusted that my story mattered. Many prayers of blessing have been prayed over you.

The Countless Prayer Warriors ... I'm afraid to list them all because I might accidentally leave someone off unintentionally. Prayer is VITAL when taking on a God sized dream. There is FIERCE spiritual warfare to warrior through. When needed I could send a quick text out to friends with specific prayer requests and I knew I could do what needed to be done with AUTHORITY and CONFIDENCE because they were speaking life and declaring God's greatness into the atmosphere.

Alexis ... girlfriend, you helped in more ways than you will ever know. Thank you is not a big enough word.

Bo and Rosanne Williams, my Pastors ... I have spent countless hours listening to your teachings and loved every second. Your hearts beat in sync with Jesus.

My readers ... thank you for taking time to read my story, now GO write yours! Your stories matter too. The world is waiting.

Heroes of the Faith ... Joyce Meyer, John and Lisa Bevere, Beth Moore, Jimmy and Karen Evans, Mark Batterson, Max Lucado, Henry Blackaby and Rick Warren have all played a part in my healing from the inside out and the strengthening of our marriage. These remarkable authors and speakers pushed through the hard, went before me and showed the way out of darkness through their Holy Spirit anointed writings and teachings.

I walk amongst giants!

CONTENTS

FOREWORD

By Bob Hamp

Every time I hear this story I hope it will turn out differently. Christie Jones has dared not just to live above a history of sexual abuse, she has chosen to talk about it!!

We should all understand that our stories matter and that nothing heals when it is hidden. Sadly, while we should all understand that very few do.

Our stories matter because it is the thing the entire human race shares in common. We all arrive somewhere in the middle of a story that God is telling. You hold one of His many chapters in your hand.

When we tell our stories, it is an invitation to others into value. It is an invitation to value the life of the writer, and hopefully for the reader to come to value their own life in a new way. If the story in your hand matters, then the story in your heart matters.

It is a particular part of this story that I always wish turned out another way.

Abuse in all of it's forms carries with it a most insidious back story.

Physical abuse, sexual abuse, psychological and emotional abuse are all soul-withering and do far more damage than many people realize. But it is still the backstory to abuse that has the most capacity to not just wither but potentially cripple the soul.

You hear hints of it in Christie's story but I feel sure that she holds back.

You see the back story to abuse is that below the surface of the violation is also mind-numbing reversal of truth that almost always follows the one moment one has the courage to bring the abuse to light.

As a counselor and a friend I have seen it again and again.

Because the context of abuse is always couched in an upside down and backwards dynamic where someone with power casts responsibility wrongly on someone without power.

In Christie's story an adult with power casts responsibility for his darkness and appetites onto a child without power. And because the fabric is made out of a misuse of power and a reversal of responsibility this little triangle almost always persists.

The abuser gains sympathy and even protection from others. The victim is asked to continue to carry the weight, even after the abuse "has stopped" and far too many onlookers expect the victim to continue to carry the weight. The expectation that the victim will carry the secret, the responsibility, and still be blamed for the abuser's sickness is the hidden story behind every case of abuse.

It is costly to bear the violation of abuse and keep it hidden.

It is costly to bring the abuse to light and lose important relationships and discover that you may not be supported by those who should protect you.

The victim of abuse has no option to live without paying a price. Their only option is to choose which price to pay.

Christie has chosen the courageous path of truth and healing.

Add these two things together.

Christie's story gives you permission to value your story. Value it!

Christie's choice to speak up is courageous and costly. Value it. And value yourself because Christie shows the way.

BOB HAMP

Counselor and Author of *Think Differently Live Differently*

INTRODUCTION

*H*ospitality is my thing. I love welcoming people of every age into my home and giving them the very best that I have to offer. When you opened this book, *A Vessel of Noble Use*, you entered into my sphere of influence. It is my heart's desire for you to feel welcomed and loved.

Mine is a beautiful journey all its own. Grab a box of tissues and your favorite drink in your favorite cup. Please feel free to dog ear, underline, circle and make notes in the margins. Be sure and date as you read. I went years without tarnishing a single page of books I read, just in case someone else wanted to read the book after me. The last few books I have read I mark up, write notes, thoughts, questions, and crease REALLY important pages. I now love to date the pages as I read, some days I read a chapter a day, some days I ponder and spend several days on a chapter.

Go at your own pace. There is no right or wrong way to read this book, just your way. I'm praying that Holy Spirit guides you, may He open your mind to receive what God wants to teach you and for YOUR heart to beat in sync with Jesus. May Jesus become your "BESTIE." This book is yours, buy another one for a friend if you want to share the contents, so they can mark up their own pages. I have several copies of my favorite books that I hand out to friends and family. They get fresh, new, clean pages without the tear stains.

Relax, take a deep breath, God is with you. Breathe Him in and let's grow together as the pages unfold.

May you join me on this journey through these pages and find that we are alike enough that my story will connect to your story and you can find healing and hope in your own circumstances. Rest assured that this journey you've chosen with me will change you, I'm certainly not the same person I was when I began it.

You are going to find me a bit quirky at times and that's okay. It took me years to have the courage to simply be me. I'd love to show you the journey that God took me through to get me comfortable enough to simply be me. There have been a lot of hard lessons along the way. I tell those I love, there are no shortcuts, but I hope to show you easier paths.

God desires for each of us to be His vessels of noble use. We are given the choice to choose Him. Choosing Him requires more than lip service. Oh, it's easy to say I am a believer in the Lord Jesus Christ as the Messiah or I am a Christian. What does it mean to be a Christian, a Christ follower? I guarantee you it's not just saying the words. You have to put some action with the words. He loves for you to step out in faith, fully trusting in Him to guide your steps, but it takes commitment from you. Are you all in or just testing the waters with Him? God knows the difference. He is one smart dude. For goodness sake, He created the universe in 6 days and only rested one day. I can take a 6-day vacation and it takes me a week to rest up from having fun.

Jesus says, "I know your deeds that you are neither cold nor hot; I wish that you were cold or hot. So, because you are lukewarm, and neither hot nor cold, I will spit you out of My mouth" (Revelations 3:15, 16; NASB). Hey let's set the world on fire for God and not leave a bad taste in His mouth. Doing this requires action.

I am stepping out in faith to tell my story because He asked me to. I asked the Lord why the world needed to hear my story. He told me that my story and my relationship with Him, Jesus, and Holy Spirit will give credibility to those who have gone before me telling their stories and will give courage to those who read mine and be inspired to tell theirs. We all have a story. My story is HIStory which is about our history together, a loving partnership. He is in me and I in Him. It excites me to be one of His Warriors willing to step completely out of my comfort zone to help set the captives free. Walking in freedom with Him is my greatest joy and I want it to be yours too. I have mental images etched in my mind of defining moments when His love broke through my grief and pain and healed my deep wounds. Talking about God, Jesus, and Holy Spirit are absolutely my favorite topics in conversations. Words that breathe life!

He's smiling and totally excited about this opportunity to tell our story, I'm shaking in my Texas boots. I am bold and courageous giving my testimony when I'm sitting in front of one or two people, but He says we are going global.

I'm taking in deep breaths while I snuggle in close to Him. He is the very air I breathe. I know that in Jesus and Jesus in me we are going to set the world on fire until it's burning bright for Him. I was created for this moment. As you read my story you will see that these words are a strong contrast from the meek, shy girl I started out as. God loves our humble beginnings.

The Apostle Paul wrote, "I can do all things through Him who strengthens me" (Philippians 4:13, NASB). Back up with me a few verses before Paul's decree and you boldly read what a vessel of noble use sets their mind on. "Finally, brethren, whatever is true, whatever is honorable, whatever is right, whatever is pure, whatever is lovely, whatever is of good repute, if there is any excellence and if anything worthy of praise, let your mind dwell on these things. The things you have learned and received and heard and seen in me, practice these things; and the God of peace shall be with you" (v. 8-9). It is my heart's desire that we all dwell in His peace and joy.

This is the story of how Jesus took a very shattered girl and made her into a vessel of noble use. I know if He can transform me He will transform you too. Snuggle in and let LOVE saturate you.

Christie Jones

CHAPTER ONE

The Past Doesn't Define You

―――――――――∽―――――――――

"To grant those who mourn in Zion, giving them a garland instead of ashes, the oil of gladness instead of mourning, the mantle of praise instead of a spirit of fainting. So they will be called oaks of righteousness, the planting of the Lord, that He may be glorified."

ISAIAH 61:3, NASB

Peeking Percy

At the time I stood 5 feet and 8 inches tall, my shoulders were slumped from carrying the weight of the world in my 26 years of life. The weight of my burdens were visible in my stature. Food helped numb and comfort me, it was my drug. My hair was blonde with the latest style, and this year I wore it short for convenience. My eyes are blue, but can easily change to green depending on what I wear and the mood I'm in. I was working 40 plus hours a week on the dayshift as a nurse at our small town hospital in the Texas panhandle. It was hard, but I was grateful to have a consistent schedule. Even my 90-year old neighbor, Percy, knew my daily schedule. He let me know this one day at the post office when we happened to be picking up our mail at the same time. He was concerned about me when he hadn't seen my bathroom light come on during the early morning hours. I assured him everything was fine, I had just stayed home sick that day but was feeling much better.

Compassion ran deep within me, but so did insecurity. It kinda freaked me out that Percy watched our house from his house across the street. He lived by himself and spent lots of sleepless nights looking out of his front window, or when the weather was good, he sat on his front porch in an old worn chair. Looking back now I feel blessed to have had a neighbor like him really care that I wasn't at work that morning. Hmm ... I guess I was watching him watching me. I'd like to think that he was saying prayers for our family, the good Lord knows we needed them.

Born Again At 26

Twenty-six is a very important age to start my story. It was the age I crashed when I was trying to do life on my own. God led me to these words which become very real to me: " ... to comfort all who mourn, and provide for those who grieve in Zion—to bestow on them a crown of beauty instead of ashes, the oil of joy instead of mournening, and a garment of praise instead of a spirit of despair.

They will be called oaks of righteousness, a planting of the Lord for the display of His splendor" (Isaiah 61:2b-3, NIV).

Even though I had been raised in church ALL of my life, I didn't KNOW Jesus personally till the age of 26 (my real birth year, 1991). I truly didn't begin living until I was 26. I wish I knew the exact day, but I didn't realize at the time how important that day would always be. God's not going to bop me on the back of the head for not remembering the date, He knows. It's written in His book and that's all that matters to me. I was forever changed that year.

Releasing the Abuse of the Past

My family moved around a lot. From the time my mother married my stepdad when I was 4 years old, till the summer going into my junior year of high school, I had moved no less than 14 times. Though I experienced the nightmare of sexual abuse—evil in every way imaginable—I was spared the degradation of actual penetration. Before I met Larry, I had only dated a handful of boys, and I saved the best of me for my husband. We were each other's first and I am so grateful that our love has stayed pure for each other.

Larry was kind and understanding as I learned to be intimate with him without a dark shadow hanging over it. My stepfather used his sickness to dominate and control. He was attracted to young girls. When I refused him he would beat me. He would tell lies about me to cover up his own lies to my mother and anyone else that questioned him. I endured perverse, dirty sexual abuse from the age of 5 until I was 16. Those times were beyond my control, but left huge scars mentally and emotionally that haunt me even now.

My mind protected me by "sealing" the most horrific memories for many years. When my relationship with Jesus deepened and I learned more about letting go of my emotions and feelings and all the junk I had bottled up from childhood, I became strong enough to handle the "sealed" memories. Growing up, I knew I didn't trust my stepdad and I absolutely hated to be alone in a room or vehicle with him. He could laugh, tell a dirty joke, or look at me in a certain way and alarms would sound throughout my body, fear and anxiety would grip me, but I couldn't explain it.

> *My mind protected me by "sealing" the most horrific memories for many years.*

We lived in a trailer house. My room was the end room, my two sisters shared a room down the hall past the bathroom from me, and my mother and stepdad's room was at the opposite end of the trailer house. My mother was pregnant with my brother and had already gone to bed. He liked tucking us in at night. The house was completely dark when he came in. He bent down to kiss me on my lips while at the same time slipping his hand under the covers and down my panties. I yelled, "NO!" loudly in the dark, it startled him. I remember feeling shocked that he thought he could really get away with that. No one asked why I yelled … That was the last time he touched me in a sexual way.

Steps To Heal

When I went into relationship with Jesus, He began slowly healing me from the inside out. I'll tell you there have been some really rough days. Who am I kidding, days? How about weeks … months. Rough months, maybe years … but there have also been some totally off the chart HALLELUJAH breakthroughs too.

First, God adjusted my music choices. No more sad, honky tonk, lying, cheating, heartbreaking love songs. He turned my love songs into worship songs that reflected new emotions I didn't even know how to describe. I had never felt love like this before. I wasn't good at it yet, but I was learning to love and to be loved. I had only known hymns. Praise and worship music ignited passion for God and Jesus, but Holy Spirit was still a mystery to me. He scared me. I hadn't been taught anything about Holy Spirit, just the name. Tears would flow freely when I was alone singing to them. Eventually, I got brave and would open my palms up to praise. Before I knew it, I was waving my arms in the air. Now 52-year-old me has a REALLY good time worshipping Jesus. Holy Spirit no longer scares me— none whatsoever.

Second, I changed what I was watching. I started watching TV evangelists. No more soap operas. I didn't need any more drama in my life. There was this older lady that I was particularly crazy about watching. I could relate to her. At the end of her shows there were opportunities to buy her teachings and I did. Joyce Meyer was the first REAL person I had ever heard talk about Jesus. She was flawed too. I loved that about her! I was working so hard to be perfect and she was the first person to introduce me to the real meaning of GRACE. Her teachings played in my car wherever I went, even to the grocery store. I listened to her while I folded laundry. I loved her style of teaching God's Word. I even went out and bought an Amplified Bible, highlighting pens, and index tabs with the names of the books like Genesis, Exodus, etc. on them so that I could find where she was teaching faster. She gave me permission to write in my Bible and I did. Ha! Whoever inherits the Bible I study out of now will totally enjoy some of my notes. I get a bit sarcastic from time to time. For instance, in Chronicles I get frustrated with the stupidity of various kings, but I also give high praises when warranted.

Third, I began building Christ centered relationships. I joined my church's ladies group. I fellowshipped. I didn't know how to be in relationship with other people and there was a learning curve. I loved learning about Jesus. Doing Bible studies in the church was the safest way I found to find like-minded people. Trust was a real issue for me and rightly so. I got adventurous and realized that the church I attended wasn't the only way to learn, I could join other Bible studies. When I stepped out is when the learning really took off. I joined a group that was learning about Redemptive Gifts that was not part of the Baptist background I had been brought up in. I love my Baptist roots, but I discovered there was more out there that I wasn't being taught that IS in the Bible. I first learned it with these ladies and that opened the door to a Joyce Meyer's Conference that radically changed me. I still have a deep friendship with the woman that taught that class, Linda Hall, and I stay in contact with a couple of the other ladies too, even though that was more than twenty years ago.

Maybe the icing on the cake is that I learned giving. Oh baby, I am here to tell you that changed everything! I learned that giving 10% of our income was non-negotiable. It started out as an experiment. I was the budgeter and there were a lot of times the income didn't look like it covered the expenses, but I made out that tithe check anyway and someway, somehow it all got covered. We weren't just tithing, we were also giving our time at church, serving. I helped in the nursery, basically anything to do with kids or youth. I even cleaned the church when asked to. Funeral meals, you name it. I sang in the choir. The more I gave, the more fulfilled I became. Richer. Content.

I enjoyed watching TV evangelists, and they inspired me to become monthly partners. I wanted to sow seeds into their ministries. I wanted to be part of what they were doing advancing God's Kingdom. My sweet husband is just as much a giver as I am. We have always prayed about where to invest the money God gives us. We are His stewards; the money is really His. If He says give, we give. Because of our obedience, He has opened up doors of opportunity that ONLY He could have opened. We are grateful and we know our source. He truly is our All in All.

There you have it. When God came into my life I started changing what I listened to, what I watched, how I built relationships, and how I invested my time and money. These were all things I had control over. Nothing I had experienced in my past could govern my present choices. I had the wonderful gift of shaping a new future that was filled with God's grace and love. The past could no longer define me.

I found that I needed less chaos inside and I needed ways to connect to God. We live in an age where there are various books by Christian authors and Christian radio and TV programs. Find what works for YOU.

———————————

Nothing I had experienced in my past could govern my present choices.

———————————

CHAPTER TWO

My Mighty Man of Valor

"Jehovah is with thee, thou mighty man of valor."

JUDGES 6:12B, ASV

Laughter Is a Gift

The first time I met this guy, he wasn't a boy but he wasn't yet a man either. I met him the first semester, my junior year of high school. I was riding around with my new friend, Toni. She was red headed and full of spunk and drove an antique red Mustang. I loved that car and the red head driving it.

Toni was casually dating Larry, they mainly just hung out from time to time. Her and I were riding around town which took a full 10 minutes round trip. She saw him parked in the middle of town so we stopped and got in with him. Toni sat between us, after the introductions it was like she didn't exist anymore. Larry wanted to know everything about me, he asked a lot of questions and I answered all of them.

He stopped dating Toni and she was fine with it …she already had someone else in mind. In the beginning he was more interested in me than I was in him. Not only was he two years older than me, he was dating my friend and I was new to town. I didn't want any trouble. I had practice at the school for the one act play almost every evening, I was part of the lighting crew. For days, he would drive by my house, showing up to hang out with me. Eventually we became friends.

A big wind storm ripped part of the roof off of the gym at the school. When Larry came to hang-out with me before practice started, I grabbed his hand and took him into the gym to show him the damage. I will never forget the moment we stood looking up at the sky through the damaged roof, in the dark, hand in hand, centered under the hole looking towards heaven. He has always held my hand so tenderly during hard times. We look towards Heaven for God's answers when everything seems dark and damaged. I didn't officially fall head over heels in love with the guy for several months.

He played short stop on a men's softball team and he was REALLY good. I could watch him play for hours … and I did! One day I was watching him do his thing and it was if he lit up. He looked brighter than anyone else on the field, I knew in my heart that I was going to marry that guy someday.

Yes, I married my high school sweetheart. Larry was the gentlest, most patient, hard-working man I had ever known. The love Larry showed me was passionate, his love was pure not perverse. He was tender and kind. So, I fell in love with the boy and ventured into our happily ever after. At this time 33 years strong with plans to keep going until death do us part.

I actually chose to date him because he made me laugh. Little did I know that his sense of humor and slogan, "Life is what you makest it, so makest it fun!" would help when times were tough in the years to come. It didn't matter that what he is saying wasn't grammatically correct, I always laugh when he says it.

He's my jokester, though his humor is never making fun of people—he has far too much integrity for that. He always creates a good time and life is never boring around this guy. Humor is a gift he carries well. I call him Jonesie—my treasured gift from the Lord. Every word he speaks to me encourages me. Okay, at least most of them. He's not perfect, but he's pretty darn near close to it in my eyes.

When we got married, Larry did whatever it took to provide for us. Pride was not an issue—he would mow yards, tend cattle, drive a wheat truck, wash cars at the local filling station, or do carpentry work. Any odd and end job that came up, he took it, adding to his full-time job. Many times, I mowed with him, brought him meals wherever he was working, or sat beside him chatting away about everything and anything to keep him company as he worked. No man ever worked harder to make a way for his family.

School of Hard Knocks

Larry's parents wanted him to go to college, but he chose instead to take an oil and gas job straight out of high school. The Texas panhandle was going through an oil boom and the pay was good. When the oil boom fizzled, because of his age and lack of experience, he was one of the first to be laid off. A friend of the family offered him a full-time job driving a propane truck, and he took it. The Lord knew he would someday manage, then own that same office.

Larry is a hard worker—his parents had instilled strong work ethics in him and his three brothers. He received an education not in the classroom, but by experience. Honestly, he is the hardest working man I know. He's in his 50s now, getting out of bed shows the toils of his years of hard labor, but he wouldn't want it any other way. He thrives when he is working with his hands and physically making things happen.

This man grabs any situation by the horns and wrestles it to the ground until he dominates it. He's my mighty man of valor, and I promise you, I had to learn to see this man the way God saw him, I prayed for it. There have been days when it was me he was figuratively wrestling to gain dominance over.

Little Miss Feisty Britches
Preaching Submission

Oh, he will tell you that we are equals in our marriage, and we do make a lot of decisions together, but God has had to teach me to let Larry lead. He appointed Larry as the head of our household and as the spiritual leader of our home. Bear with me on allowing me to insert Ephesians 5:22-30 here, but I need to read this often, sometimes daily. I'm very feisty. If you never have heard it in the Message version before, you've got to hear it now. I love how it's stated:

Wives, understand and support your husbands in ways that show your support to Christ.

(Hmmm … I had to learn to let Larry lead. We couldn't even dance together I was always wanting to lead. We dance beautifully now because Jesus has been schooling me with some major lessons on following, going with the flow, letting go of control, and synchronizing.)

The husband provides leadership to his wife the way Christ does to his church, not by domineering but by cherishing.

(I must say that God gave Larry extra patience and tolerance … did I mention I am a handful?)

So just as the church submits to Christ as he exercises such leadership, wives should likewise submit to their husbands.

Husbands, go all out in your love for your wives, exactly as Christ did for the church—a love marked by giving, not getting. Christ's love makes the church whole.

(In my opinion, a husband's love makes the family whole.)

His words evoke her beauty. Everything he does and says is designed to bring the best out of her, dressing her in dazzling white silk, radiant with holiness. And that is how husbands ought to love their wives. They're really doing themselves a favor—since they're already "one" in marriage.

Don't you absolutely love how the Message Bible translates these verses? Larry has always loved me more than I loved myself. He honestly brings out the best in me. I've practiced many things on him, take my cooking for example. I'm a great cook now because he didn't die (make that, I didn't kill him) from comparing my cooking to his mother's more than a handful of times. He quickly learned to compliment my cooking. Eventually, along the way I rose up to that standard. His mama really is one of the best cooks I know. Poor guy had to endure a lot of training along the way, but he survived and by the looks of him, he has definitely thrived!

Wise Choices

Before the company layoff, Larry used earnings from his oil and gas job to purchase a quaint little house on Main Street. The first time he showed me the house I was stung by a wasp. I don't like critters and the house was full of them—which decreased the odds of me revisiting the house often tremendously! Soon after we started dating, the house burnt to the ground. Lightning struck it! Yes, it was the strangest of strange phenomenons. He hadn't even had it long enough to officially live in it full time. For several months, he had slowly been filling the house with dishes and furniture he was collecting from here and there. I had only been in it a couple of times before it burned.

Ironically, Larry was a volunteer fireman, and he helped put the fire out that destroyed his first piece of property. When the address came over the scanner he knew it was his house that was on fire. I was the first person he went to after the fire was extinguished. He smelled heavily of smoke. Soot was smeared across his face and his hands were black from sifting through the ashes.

I remember standing outside when he pulled up at my house. I knew something had to be wrong because he was severely late picking me up for a date and that wasn't like him. When I saw him, all I knew to do was hold him close to my heart. Larry says he felt my heart beating and heard my words of encouragement and knew in his own heart that it would be okay.

I went with him to tell his parents, as if they didn't already know. In a small town news—good and bad—travels faster than the speed of light. I remember how awesome and encouraging his parents were about the whole situation. Larry's dad had the bright idea to clear off the burnt debris and build a new house from the ground up. I knew that man could do anything he put his mind to. One of my favorite sayings about Larry and his dad was that Larry hung the moon, but his dad straightened it. I can literally see this picture in my head whenever I think of them. His dad is a genius at anything he put his mind to.

Father and son soon began clearing off the burnt debris. The house they built measured 1200 square feet, with three bedrooms and two full baths. Larry had been approved for an FHA Loan with a low interest rate. Through the summer his best friend from high school, Paul, helped. This was no ordinary home, if a board needed

2 nails they put in 4. Only quality materials were used. Because it was located on Main Street, everyone in town kept a close eye on its progress.

Larry always found time for us even during the long hours of building. I'm smiling just remembering Mrs. Wiley, one of the teachers, telling Larry he could be my date for the sweetheart banquet but this would be his LAST year. He had attended all four of his high school years and one of mine. He was two years older than me so I understood her point—he was getting too old for high school dances!

CHAPTER THREE

Finding Me

"*For we are His workmanship, created in Christ Jesus for good works, which God prepared beforehand so that we would walk in them.*"

EPHESIANS 2:10, NASB

Doing What I'm Told

It was time for me to make a decision about my future. Both Larry and my mother really wanted me to go to college, but I didn't want to leave Larry. I had grown very attached to him. Mother suggested I go to nursing school in Lubbock and live with my grandmother, Mom Melton. I went. I typically did what I was told to do.

Although I was 18, I lacked the confidence and decisiveness to make my own decisions. I was always afraid of "screwing up." I wanted to be somebody, I just didn't know who. As the oldest of four, taking care of people came naturally to me. I was always in charge of caring for my two younger sisters. My baby brother came along when I was 16 years old. He was spoiled by all of us looking after him. So, being a nurse sounded like a good idea. I didn't have any ideas of my own, so why not? There was a need for nurses and they got paid well.

The Jitters

I was accepted into the LVN nursing program at South Plains Junior College, so in 1984 I packed up and moved to Lubbock. I applied and qualified for a Pell Grant. The remainder of what I needed to pay for school was covered with a student loan. The nursing campus was located in a building downtown. I was so nervous about being on my own that I wrote my checking account number in the spaces where I should have written my social security number! It fit perfectly and I didn't know any better. Boy did that take a lot of time to fix when I realized what I did wrong … days later—clearly a "blonde" moment.

Treasured Memories

I moved in with Mom Melton. She lived in a small, two-bedroom trailer house on the outskirts of town. Though I was named after her, the two of us hardly knew each other. Every Saturday night we ate hamburgers and drank a Coke from a bottle while watching Lawrence Welk. My mother must have gotten this tradition from Mom Melton because we did the same thing when I was growing up except we watched shows like *Charlie's Angels* or *The Bionic Woman*.

I didn't have a car so Mom Melton was gracious and shared hers. It was a very old car that barely got from Point A to Point B, but it did the trick. My Aunt Mary and Uncle David, whom I treasured, lived close by and kept a close eye on the two of us.

Remembering them brings back so many sweet memories. David was mother's youngest brother, they were the two youngest kids of seven. My mother's name was Judy. David and Judy could fight like no other, but they were each other's best friend. David was a big ole teddy bear, he could easily make my mother laugh. There were times he was the ONLY one that could make her laugh.

Uncle David and Aunt Mary quit school and got married when they were in their mid-teens. These two might not have been considered book smart, but they were street smart. The two of them built a successful insulation business from the ground up. I grew up close to them and we spent a lot of time together. Their sons (my cousins) Todd and Steve were like brothers to me. If I needed anything, especially love and laughter, all I had to do was hang out in their kitchen, it was the best place to be. The most dangerous place was in a vehicle with my cousin Steve. He was two years younger than me and could scare the living daylights out of me when I bravely went anywhere with him.

Smell Mail

These were the days before email and texting—we didn't even have cell phones, so Larry and I wrote each other letters daily and mailed them through the post office. I would spray my perfume on the envelope and remarkably, it could still be smelled three days later when it arrived in his mailbox. I'm sure the post office workers got a kick out of our letter exchanges.

He sprayed his cologne, Polo by Ralph Lauren or Grey Flannel on the letters he wrote to me. It's funny I can remember the exact scents he wore, but can't recall for the life of me what I wore.

I went to the mailbox located by the road in front of Mom Melton's trailer house every day except Sunday. The mail didn't run on Sundays. We didn't even care that the letter we were experiencing was already three-day-old news. I wish we still had those treasured letters. A pesky rat that obviously loved smell good, mushy love letters, made his home in the box we stored them. Obviously, the old storage building we kept our keepsakes in was NOT critter proof!

Kept Promises

Before I left for college, Larry gave me a promise ring. I asked him the other day why he didn't give me an engagement ring and he said he couldn't afford an engagement ring at the time. He wanted me to focus on getting an education. He knew if he had asked me to marry him that I would have, and he wasn't yet ready for the full-time commitment that came with marriage. He knew our love for each other was strong, but we could also fight like cats and dogs and then thirty minutes later be making up.

Being apart wasn't easy, I mailed him back his ring more than once … come to think of it, maybe it was a good thing he didn't spend a fortune on an engagement ring. It never got lost in the mail, but it made several round trips. Larry would mail it right back to me because by the time he got the ring in the mail we had already made up over a long-distance phone call. It typically took it a week to make the round trip from Lubbock to our hometown and then back to Lubbock.

Life with my fiesty self has always been a bit intense.

Worth It

Long distance phone calls were expensive in the 80s. I worked part time as a hostess at a steakhouse, which was great with my school schedule and I was paid the giant salary of $3.50 an hour. On slow nights, I sat near my hostess post with my books studying for the next exam. I paid $100 a month to Mom Melton for food, rent, and to call Larry a couple of times a week. Though Larry had little time for chats or writing letters, he made the time for me. I am amazed at how much attention he has always given me.

After work and on weekends was all he had to build this house, they had a deadline of finishing it in 6 months … and they did. At the time I felt neglected and alone, but looking at the situation 33 years later, it's clear that he worked his tail off to build a house and to love me. God gave that boy an extra anointing and a special love to help heal all my past hurts and wounds. Somehow the two of them thought I was worth it.

This Chick Was Flying … But Not High!

My heart wasn't into becoming a nurse. In high school, I had made all As, now I was failing Anatomy. Making friends was easy, one of the perks of moving so often. I had two girlfriends, Kim and Tammy. We were all three the same age and we hung out with each other in class. When I wasn't working we hung out at Kim's apartment with her roommate from high school.

Kim and Tammy took me to my first concert for my 19th birthday at the Lubbock Coliseum on the Texas Tech Campus. We saw the Go Go Girls and sang "We Got The Beat" at the top of our lungs. That's the first time I smelled the strange scent of marijuana. It did not appeal to me and I never smoked weed or did drugs.

My drug was always food. In high school and even in college my addiction was completely hidden. My metabolism helped keep it hidden.

Kim and Tammy weren't doing too well with nursing school either. We were failing together which was comforting to us, but clearly not a good thing to have in common. Time spent with them helped me adapt to being away from Larry. I rarely felt homesick for my family. I had really wanted to escape my family life and living in Lubbock made that mission accomplished.

Being in Lubbock was somehow God's plan, I experienced freedom for the first time. I made mistakes but they were all mine,

I owned them, nobody blamed them on me. In that season, Mom Melton became one of the greatest role models in my life. She spoke LIFE into me. Distance did make the heart grow stronger between Jonesie and me, that saying is true. I didn't recognize that the path I was walking had been created for me by Him—prepared for me in advance (Eph. 2:10)—but God's handiwork was there just the same.

His hand was on me,
leading and guiding.

CHAPTER FOUR

The Hard Truth

---

*"If you hold to my teaching, you are really My disciples.
Then you will know the truth and the truth will set you free."*

JOHN 8:31-32, NASB

Hypocrisy vs. Authenticity

Wanting to fly the nest and make a life separate from your family is typical, but for me there were deeper reasons beyond the natural quest for independence. I wanted to escape for darker reasons. I longed for complete detachment. I had endured years of abuse from a stepdad who could play the part of being a man of the church easily to the public eye, but behind closed doors was evil to the core. His abuse was sexual in nature and when I was what he called "rebellious" to his needs, he would beat me with a belt till I was black and blue.

My first memory of being uncomfortable around him was when I was about 5 years old. I was left alone with him because my baby sister was sick and in the hospital. I woke up in his bed completely afraid of him, completely hating him. The experience was so horrendous it haunted me. There were many incidents throughout the years, the worst ones I sealed deep in the core of my being just to cope and be able to survive, but I could never escape the effects of the wounds. It has taken a lot of time to be able to unseal those memories. When a wound heals the scar left behind is permanent, but the scars are a reminder that healing has taken place. I know that God heals, He can and will make it beautiful.

Two of a Kind

While living in Lubbock with Mom Melton, the phone rang one evening well after dark. I got up from bed to answer the phone. My sister was on the other end. She was in tears as she told me she had talked to Larry about what was going on at home and he told her to tell mother and me about it. She chose to confide only in me. Our stepdad had been sexually abusing her as well, as far back as she could remember. My mother married him when I was four and she was less than a year old.

She didn't go into details. I didn't want to know the details … and I didn't have a lot of details to tell her having blocked most of them from my mind. Mostly as she talked feelings surfaced and I had a deep "knowing." I could only tell her that I knew without a shadow of a doubt that she was telling the truth. I believed every word of what she said. I was surprised! I thought I was the only one he had messed with. I hurt deeply for her.

This man was very good at controlling us all. I feared him and rightfully so, he did exactly what he said he would. When he told me that he would beat me black and blue, he did. I have cousins and others that saw the bruises but in the 60s and 70s no one did anything about it. My sister made me swear that I wouldn't tell anyone about our conversation. I knew that was a promise I couldn't keep, I just didn't know how or when I was going to share it.

Prayer Warrior

Mom Melton heard my end of that after dark conversation. Her room wasn't far from where I sat by the phone. As I walked by her room thinking she was asleep, she called me in to sit on the edge of her bed. She comforted me by saying that she always suspected he was harming us, but could never prove it. She explained to me that she had tried to talk to my mother many times about her concerns. She told me that she risked not ever seeing us again every time she tried to talk to my mother, but having only her intuition and no proof she could never get through to her.

She prayed many prayers for us girls and even gave me specific times in our lives she was concerned about our welfare … and she was right about those times. It was comforting to hear that she did the only thing she knew to do, pray. "Obviously," I thought, "those did no good." But I was wrong. Prayers live.

When she prayed them God heard. God had a plan of restoration and blessing from the very beginning. Looking back now, I see Him do what only He could do throughout some really tough times in my life.

Sagging Shoulders & Unsealing the Vault

Life continued. I started carrying the burden of my sister's abuse along with my own secrets, but kept silent. Mom Melton and I never talked about it again after that night. I did what I did best—sealed it, but because of my maturity and because it had hurt my sister, this awareness was harder to keep in the deep recesses of my mind. It would pop out and demand my attention.

Mom Melton's car couldn't be trusted to make a road trip. My friend Kim lived in Childress which was a little over an hour from our hometown. She went home most weekends so when I could get off from my job at the steakhouse I would ride with her to Childress and Larry would come and pick me up. Otherwise it was a four-hour trip from Lubbock. It took a lot of coordinating to make things happen, but I had the mindset that if there was a way, I would find it, and I did. Larry and I talked about everything, including my latenight conversation with my sister and Mom Melton. I had told him early in our relationship that my step dad wasn't a good person, but it took a long time for me to bit by bit trust him enough to tell him about the feelings, the fears, and the concerns I had about my stepfather.

Gut feelings were really all I could relay … until recently. Now that memories have slowly begun to unseal, I totally understand why a little girl couldn't handle them. As a fifty-year old woman, I mourned and grieved over what had occurred as if it just happened. Keeping the memories sealed had also kept them fresh, sharp as a knife and able to cut deep.

Freedom Ministries

Our dear friend Beth was a pastor at Gateway Church in Southlake, TX. She was involved with Freedom Ministries with a guy named Bob Hamp who had his own unique style of Christian counseling. Larry had gone to school with Beth so we knew she didn't believe in wrong teachings. Beth would post information on Facebook about Bob's teachings and I loved his perspective. When his book *Think Differently, Live Differently Keys to a Life of Freedom* came out in 2010, I bought it and highlighted key words and sentences that resonated in me, wrote notes, dog eared the pages, and even gathered a group of ladies from my church to study the book. We went through it chapter by chapter. I was taking baby steps in the right direction. God was preparing my heart to find healing.

I woke up one morning knowing it was an important day that I would never forget. I spent time in prayer and reading scripture. I trusted that whatever I went through, He was in control and I had complete peace. I dressed for my workout, grabbed my laptop computer, and dropped off my youngest at school. On the way to the gym I heard Him say, "It's time."

"Time for what, Lord?" I asked.

"It's time to unlock what has been sealed. Do you trust me dear one?" He continued.

Part of me was actually relieved that I would finally see what the TRUTH was. I honestly wanted to believe that all my fears were just childhood insecurities. On this day, at that moment I had a true wake-up call from a slumber I didn't even know I was in until after I was jolted fully awake.

I parked my Jeep in the church parking lot across from the gym and took deep breaths in. "You are the very air I breathe," I said to myself.

I pushed my seat back and turned my computer on. With my eyes closed I typed every emotion, every detail, and every word of my conversation with Jesus as we unsealed a memory that was worse than I could have ever imagined. There were moments of gasping for air as tears cascaded down my cheeks and saturated my shirt. In the toughest parts Jesus would ask me if I could see Him in the room with me as a child. I looked and He WAS there, He never left my side.

All at once I knew WHY I didn't trust my stepdad, why I feared him, why I knew every word my sister said in that phone call late that night at Mom Melton's was true. The memory was so vivid and clear, it had been sealed in a time capsule that only Jesus could have opened when the time was right.

"Why now Lord?" I asked Him.

"You weren't mature enough to remember before. You were an innocent child. I protected the most powerful part of you, my precious one, for such a time as this," He whispered to my heart. "There are more memories we will unseal together. You will grow stronger and feel them less deeply."

I took that in, giving Him the fear and uncertainty that rose at the thought of more.

He waited until I was ready to hear Him and continued, "Your wounds will heal from the inside out as we open up and reveal truth upon truth. You will gain momentum as you gain back territory that the enemy has stolen. Your words will matter and the truth will prevail. You are more powerful now than you were as a child. Your roots are strong in Me, dear one. All is well."

I sat in that parking lot and weeped. Physically, I felt as weak as a newborn kitten. Emotionally, I felt dirty and nasty, defiled by what had been done to me. I had trusted my mother's husband to be my daddy, to take care of me, but instead he used me to satisfy his own flesh then physically threw me down a hallway when I screamed in defiance at what he had done to me.

Processing

Jesus and I had a lot of lengthy conversations for days. I had to fully process the images that were now so clear in my mind, the new emotions. I mourned and grieved. Hard. Then a strength arose in me. I realized that I wasn't the same me I was before the memory was unsealed. I was more powerful. I was stronger. The truth really did set me free.

I allowed Larry to read the details of what I wrote as I saw the unsealed memory for the first time. It was powerful and graphic. Detailed. Larry was sweet, loving and gentle with me. It was as if he was the very arms of Jesus holding me and wrapping me in unconditional love. The man who did this is still alive, very active in the church in the small town he lives in, and fully denies any wrong doing to me or to my sister. I don't know if he has done this to anyone else over the years or not. Men who behave this way often do not usually limit their activities to one or two victims.

God is a God of justice. He balances the scales.[1] When evil rears its ugly head, then God balances the scales. In my life, I've seen Him tip the scales more heavily in His favor with many blessings. Throughout the Bible we see the justice He rendered when Lucifer was cast down from Heaven, how Jesus had to redeem us all because of the fall of man in the Garden of Eden with Adam and Eve. God ultimately prevails when an injustice is done. Jehovah Mishpat means God of Justice. This verse gives me great peace:

"Even though a person sins and gets by with it hundreds of times throughout a long life, I'm still convinced that the good life is reserved for the person who fears God, who lives reverently in his presence, and that the evil person will not experience a "good" life. No matter how many days he lives, they'll all be as flat and colorless as a shadow—because he doesn't fear God."

ECCLESIASTES 8:12-*13*

Endnote

1.   Proverbs 16:11, Job 31:6, Proverbs 11:1.

CHAPTER FIVE

Life is What You Make It

"But the fruit of the Spirit is love, joy, peace, patience, kindness, goodness, faithfulness, gentleness and self-control ..."

GALATIANS 5:22-23, NASB

I had tough days, but life wasn't all a struggle. God began tipping the scales in my favor, blessing my life by filling me with delight. Though I had not yet come to know Jesus as my Savior, Larry had. Holy Spirit flowed freely through him and therefore, touched me too. I saw in Larry a zeal for life. I laughed because Larry laughed. Watching Larry's relationship with God, I saw Holy Spirit as crazy, fun and adventurous. There is nothing flat and colorless about Holy Spirit—life is lived in Technicolor when He is allowed to flow freely. The two of them together were contagious.

Big Bass

Larry's humor has always gotten us through tough stuff. He has taught me how to not take life so seriously ALL the time. It blows my mind how Larry can easily hand over his problems to God, let them go, and trust that everything is really going to be okay. He does what he can do and then let's go and lets God do what He can do. They have a great partnership.

Larry flourishes outdoors, he fully enjoys God's creations. His favorite hobby has always been fishing and this is one of the ways we laugh and relax. We pack snacks—mainly sunflower seeds, sandwiches, chips and a sipping drink like sweet tea or Coke—head to the nearest pond and fish. He believes in catch and release, so it's all about the challenge of catching the "Big One" and then releasing it back into the water to see another day or year. He's always preferred catching Largemouth Bass. The big guys get smarter and aren't easily caught … you know, like "Walter" the humongous trout from the movie *On Golden Pond*.

Christie's 101 on Culling Perch

A few years ago, we were invited to a Perch Rodeo at the family pond of one of Larry's co-workers. This pond was being overtaken by Perch, and they decided that thinning them out was a much needed task to reset the eco system, so why not make it a competition and have fun doing it?

They set a time limit of one hour. Whoever caught the most Perch had bragging rights as the winner. Couples could work together and Larry and I were a team. We were to get as many out of that pond as possible within the hour set time and have fun doing it. There were no rules as to the methodology. Larry's choice of bait was grasshoppers and live worms so we arrived early to collect the bait. Tall grass and weeds were everywhere so the grasshoppers were not hard to find. That man could sneak up on grasshoppers and catch them with his bare hands. Me ... I just watched and laughed.

The cattle used the pond as their water source so there were cow patties everywhere. For those of you who aren't from the country, cow patties are piles of cow poop that come out of the cow semi soft while the cow is standing still and it pools into a circle below its behind. It's ALWAYS best to stay away from fresh piles! Larry knew to kick over the dried out cow patties and there would be live worms exposed in the soil. He filled an old coffee can up right before the horn sounded to start the rodeo.

I had my lawn chair set up next to the water's edge, away from cow patties and tall grass. Larry would bait my line, I'd throw it out and immediately catch a perch. He would take off the live fish and put it in a bucket. He was casting and reeling them in as well. He was hot and sweaty from his workout of baiting and reeling in while I sat in relative comfort and just had fun. He never sat down.

If we caught a bass or catfish it was released back into the water. At the end of the hour the horn was sounded and the Perch were counted. Larry won! He gained the bragging rights for that year. The Perch were thrown over the dam into the woods for the wildlife to enjoy.

101 on Texas Caviar

The meal afterwards was just as much fun. Everyone brought fish from their home freezers they had caught other places like Foss Lake. Calf fries are always a staple at these shindigs. Calf fries (sometimes called mountain oysters) are balls (testicles), approximately the size of walnuts up to the size of an avocado, from a young bull that are peeled, breaded in flour (sometimes a beer batter) and deep fried. Many steakhouses in the Lone Star State of Texas have them on their menus. Next time you are in Texas, check it out for yourself. Though they are a delicacy in this neck of the woods, personally I can't get past my mind to let my taste buds experience the cuisine. My kitchen sink has been full of mountain oysters on more than a dozen occasions. Larry and his brothers have always been the ones to clean and put them in freezer bags, CLEARLY MARKED. For the record ... I don't clean fish either.

A fish fry is not a success amongst the locals unless calf fries are also part of the cuisine.

101 on Bulls vs. Steers

There is a difference between a bull and steer and a heifer and a cow. I'm not sure how important this is to you, but around here this is need-to-know information. This is my interpretation: young bulls that have been castrated are referred to as steers from that moment on. A cow is a female that has borne one or more calves, a heifer is a female that has never had a calf. Why would anyone WANT to castrate bulls on purpose? To put it in a nutshell (pun intended), ranchers prefer to manage their breeding by only selecting the finest bulls to build their herds with, the rest of the guy cattle are made into steers. Bulls can be mean and hard to handle, steers are less aggressive. I've been with Larry when he had to use an old farm truck to deal with a bull that had wondered to the ladies side of the field when it wasn't planned. That fella added a few more dents to that old farm truck as he was corralled to the fenced in area where he needed to be.

Bullfrog Jonesie

For decades, Larry has had permission to fish in private ponds throughout the county. There are a flood of memories and places we have fished. One of my favorites is when he worked hard to catch a bullfrog perched on a lily pad in the middle of a pond. We heard that frog as soon as we got out of the pick-up. It was like he was daring us to find him. The clouds were building into a storm far out in the distance so it was a race with nature and a fun challenge to find the frog before lightening got too close. There he was, all big and fat with bulging eyes, croaking loudly. I pulled out my chair to get all comfortable, I knew this was a showdown I didn't want to miss. Larry opened up his tackle box, chose just the right hook, and the most life like artificial worm that would entice the frog to eat it. From the bank of the pond, he stood at the water's edge. There wasn't a lot of brush or debris between him and the monster bullfrog. He was on a mission, poised and focused. It took a couple of casts before he practically hit the frogs mouth. When that huge bullfrog chomped down on his bait the fight was on. You'd a thought he was in a rodeo with all the whooping and hollering going on. That frog was all over the place, he wasn't going to be reeled in easily. I laughed so hard I almost peed my shorts. He got that big guy in, they looked eye to eye and then he removed the hook from his mouth and set him free. The rain came and we ran to the pick-up laughing the whole way. That was the catch of the day. He's caught several since then. He loves a good challenge, and I don't mind the show.

Bopping Snakes

This man can catch anything he put his mind to. Snakes, on the other hand are a different story. We don't like snakes. I've seen him bop them on top of the head with the end of his rod to keep them away from the boat. Oh gosh, I've been on the lake with Larry, up a secluded creek with eerie tree branches overhead and a snake fall out of the tree right in front of us. We both screamed like girls and almost fell in the water scrambling to get the trolling motor in the water to get us out of there. I've also had to have ticks removed from walking in grass knee high. We both love experiencing nature but when I get to Heaven I've got a few questions to ask God, such as why did He create snakes, ticks, biting flies, mosquitoes, and wasps?

Larry's Baby

I love fishing with Christie. It is one of our favorite times together and has brought us a great deal of joy. In 1990 we bought our first boat. It was an aluminum, 17' boat with a 50 hp Mercury motor, Bass Tracker Tournament TX. I bought it from an elderly widow who lived in the country. She had the boat stored in an old wooden shed with no door. Every time I filled her propane tank up I'd go look at it. I asked her soon after her husband died if she would sell it. She always said no. For three years, I had my eye on that boat. One day I was admiring it in the shed after I had filled her propane tank, she came out and asked if I was still interested in buying it.

"Heck ya," I said, "How much do you want for it?"

She priced it to me for $3,500.00 which was about half of what a new one would have cost me. I went to my banker and he loaned me the money to be paid off in two years. I was in hog heaven. I polished that aluminum boat till it shined.

One time me and Christie took that boat to Foss Lake in Oklahoma. The water got so rough while we were out in the middle of that lake that it felt like we were floating in a little wash tub in the middle of an ocean. I couldn't get Christie to go fishing with me in a big lake again in that little boat. I have to admit I was pretty scared that day myself.

For three years, I took that aluminum boat to fishing tournaments, one each month throughout the summer. Our Bass Club consisted of about 20 guys I'd grown up around most of my life. The days and the time I spent with two of my brothers, best buddy Paul from high school, and these guys was worth every penny I paid for that boat.

Some trips we slept in our boats, or on picnic tables, or in the back of our pick-up trucks. It wasn't worth spending the money on a motel room. We pre-fished the lake the evening before the tournament till dark then grilled steaks, potatoes, and had Bush's baked beans around a campfire telling jokes and wild stories till late. At 4:00 am we would all be lined up sitting in our boats drinking coffee waiting for the sun to come out. We fished till 3:00 in the afternoon, loaded up our boats onto our trailers and weighed in our catches. Everybody paid their $20 entry fee. $15 of it went towards paying first and second place winners. $5 of everyone's entry fee went to the person who caught the biggest bass that day. There was a couple of times I got first place and Big Bass. I kept a scrapbook of all the tournaments. The stats were put in the local newspaper. We were celebrities!

In 1993, Christie and I stopped at a dealership just to look at new boats. I walked in and saw the prettiest bass boat I had ever seen, a white Javelin DC180 with black and red pin stripes and a 150 hp Johnson motor. I told that salesman there was no way I could afford a boat like that. He made me a payment plan I couldn't turn down, so for 10 years I mailed him $185.03 and I had that boat for 22 years.

I nicknamed Larry's boat "Baby" because he babied that boat. Every time he came home from having it on the water he would vacuum it out and polish it with Lemon Pledge before he even kissed me hello. I really loved being out on the water with him in that boat. Skidding across the water at 60 mph thrilled me.

CHAPTER SIX

Being Drawn In

"You did not choose me, but I chose you and appointed you so that you might go and bear fruit-fruit that will last- and so that whatever you ask in my name the Father will give you."

JOHN 15:16, NIV

Radical Changes

Cancer. I hate that word. Mother was diagnosed with this dreadful disease while I was living in Lubbock attending school. It had began in her cervix then spread throughout her female organs. She had a radical hysterectomy at the age of 38, and went through radiation therapy afterwards. I was so troubled by it that I couldn't stay focused on school. I knew that I was failing Anatomy, so I opted for an "Incomplete" instead of a "Fail." I quit nursing school, said goodbye to my friend Tammy, left my job, hugged Mom Melton goodbye, and headed back home.

Treasured Memory

Leaving Mom Melton was hard, she had become precious to me. The time I spent with that incredible prayer warrior was an important part of God drawing me into relationship with Him. My stepdad had always made negative comments about her being a holy roller, and practically blind. He made her out to be a weak old lady, but this woman was sharp. I often walked past her room, saw her sitting on her bed with her Bible open talking to Jesus like he was sitting in the room right beside her. Watching her touched me down deep in the core of my being and became a treasured memory. This weak, old lady was mighty, her best friend was the Creator of the Universe. Mom Melton's physical eyes might have been weak, but she could see keenly into the spiritual realm.

Unwelcomed Choices

I packed what I could into Kim's car and left Lubbock. When I got to Childress I spent the night with Kim and called my mother to pick me up. I didn't consult anyone about my decision and it was a surprise to everyone that I had quit school ... and no one was happy with my choice.

I felt like I was the oldest, it was my responsibility to help out at home, my mother needed me—at least that's what I told myself and anyone that asked. My true motive was that my heart couldn't stand being away from Larry any longer. I quickly realized that he was busy, there wasn't much time for me. He had a deadline.

Building for Our Future

Larry had taken out a loan through the FHA to build the house. He had to get his lumber from the local lumber yard and they were willing to carry the bill for a month before being paid. The FHA wouldn't disperse checks until they inspected certain stages of building, so as each stage was completed and passed inspection, he would use FHA money to pay his bill at the lumber company. It was quite a juggle for him and I was proud of how he managed things.

The owner of the lumber yard knew Larry well and trusted him. Larry took that trust seriously and worked hard to meet his deadlines and keep his bills paid on time. His word and his reputation were important to him. Of course I was important to him too, but for that season his attention had to be focused on getting the house finished. Our future together was waiting on the completion of a home where we could begin it.

Encounter with Wisdom

I got a job as a nurse's aide at the local retirement center which was within walking distance from my home. I was making bad choices, but that didn't seem to change God's plans for me. Though I wasn't aware of it, He was still setting up opportunities to draw me towards Him. I was stubborn and super whiney (kind of like the Israelites), yet God kept His favor on me. It had to be because of Mom Melton's prayers, because I certainly wasn't talking to God. One patient I had the pleasure of caring for was a sweet lady who loved Jesus like Mom Melton did.

Mrs. D. kept her room immaculate, she had personal pieces of furniture and belongings placed throughout. When you walked into her room it was more like walking into her home, not simply a room off a hallway of a building. When I checked in on her and helped her get ready for the day it was easy to forget she was in a "facility." Mrs. D. would light up with a smile every time I walked through her door. This particular day I stood outside in the hallway observing her. She had her Bible opened in her lap, with her head tilted upwards, eyes open, talking to Jesus. She was at peace talking to Him, and there was love in her tone and in her words. I recognized this same scene with Mom Melton.

I had been in church practically all my life and never understood the Bible.

As I walked in Mrs. D. asked me to sit on the bed beside her. She began telling me all about what she had been reading in the Bible. I was deeply perplexed, I had been in church practically all my life and never understood the Bible. In my opinion, it was a boring book that was severely outdated. "Don't you ever get bored reading it?" I asked.

"Sweet child," she replied, "this morning I was thanking Jesus for His Word … this Bible of His never gets old or boring. I've been reading it almost all my life." Her voice was kind and her eyes were soft as she spoke, "Even at 90-years-old He teaches me new things."

I sat beside her feeling the peace in her room. Such calm, an unforced rhythm of grace. Her words stirred something in my mind, though it would be years before my heart would follow. God is patient.

Here were two beautiful examples of women that never got bored with Him. They were my first encounters of what a godly woman truly looked like. Mom Melton and Mrs. D. were beautifully engraved into my soul—my first glimpse of vessels of noble use. They influenced me just by simply being themselves, nothing more, nothing less. I was still in the darkness, but they showed me a glint of light.

———————

I sat beside her feeling the peace in her room. Such calm, an unforced rhythm of grace. Her words stirred something in my mind, though it would be years before my heart would follow. God is patient

———————

CHAPTER SEVEN

Not My Original Plan

"'For My thoughts are not your thoughts, nor are your ways My ways,' declares the Lord."

ISAIAH 55:8, NASB

Smitten by Christie

I had plenty of fun friendships with girls, but I didn't have a history of dating. I thought Christie was beautiful—long legged and tall—she gave me butterflies the first time I met her, and I still have those same butterflies in my tummy when I'm around her. It's a continual warm, fuzzy feeling. When we first met I started stalking her, sneaking by her house when I was on my motorcycle, just hoping to get a glimpse of her.

Jonesie, it hasn't always been warm and fuzzy ...

Christie and I have had our fair share of disagreements, though mostly minor ones. She is stubborn, but making up has always been good. We wanted everyone else to leave us alone so that it was just us. We couldn't get enough of each other. When we were dating, I'd drop her off at her house and then call her 4 minutes later when I got home. We've had some intense disagreements too. One particular time she was so mad at me that she opened the door of my pickup ... while it was moving ... and jumped out. She hit the pavement with the back of her head. We were in a residential section, and not driving very fast so I guess she thought she could just step out and run from me. I held her for about an hour and a half afterwards. I never knew when she would impulsively do things and it scared me. The fight was about me taking her home when she didn't want to go home. I had to work the next day, I had responsibilities and needed to take her home so I could go to bed. Love doesn't pay the bills. Life with Christie was anything but dull and boring. She was and is unpredictable, it keeps life interesting!

Like a moth to a flame, Larry was drawn to me from the moment we met. I beat to my own drum, and he'd never met anyone else like me. He loved to hear me laugh and he knew life with me would never be boring, and he was right. Oh, the things I talked him into! If I got an idea in my head I was determined to see it through come hell or high water. Larry had grown up with three brothers, he knew nothing about girls, but loved the challenge of trying to figure me out. Sometimes my stubbornness was infuriating to him and sometimes it was inspiring. He didn't understand my mood swings … I didn't even understand them, but being loved by this man is one of the very best things about my life.

Out of Place and Out of Sorts

I'm telling you, I was a handful in my younger years. In my defense, there was a lot going on at home that Larry didn't fully know about and it took me a long time to trust him enough to tell. I lived in a very stressful atmosphere. You already know that my mother was going through health issues, and my stepdad was abusive. Our house was pretty small for a family of 6. I had already been on my own in Lubbock, and going back home to close quarters was hard. I didn't fit in. I was out of place physically and out of sorts emotionally.

I still had grant money to go to school and my school loan was still active, so I went back to school—South Plains College in Levelland, about 4 hours from home. This time around I took classes like shorthand, basic computer, an English course, a math course, and a speech class. The campus was about 30 minutes from Lubbock. I could visit Mom Melton and my Aunt Mary and Uncle David, whom I treasured, were close enough as well. I had graduated high school with Larry's brother and my future sister in law and they went to Levelland. They had one semester behind them, and were starting their second. They let me ride home with them whenever they made the trip.

It wasn't as hard to leave home this time around. Larry was busy building the house, and it didn't feel right being back. In fact, nothing felt right. I was restless.

Keeping It Shallow

I decided to re-invent myself. I had a new start in a new place. This time I would live in the dorm. My roommate was the dorm monitor. She was serious and bland. Not my choice! Having the Resident Assistant as a roommate meant that I never got in trouble for going against the rules. I had to be super alert to the rules and adhere closely to them ... she made *sure* of that. (Can you see me rolling my eyes?) I don't even remember her name, the last day of classes was the last time I saw her and that was a very good thing.

Ziggy was a popular cartoon character at the time. He was super cute and had a fun sense of humor, I made him my personal mascot and liked wearing hats that sported Ziggy. I wanted to laugh more and feel less—Ziggy helped me do that.

Though I made friends easily, I should clarify that I ALWAYS kept relationships shallow. I didn't let ANYONE into the deep side of me. I didn't think anyone could handle the deep side and I was NOT going to put myself at risk of exposing too much. Most of the friends I made were gentle, kind, and if they were going to hang around me they had to be fun loving.

Rebel Friends in Low Places

Serena was a bit of a rebel without a cause. She led a small band of us to go past boundaries. My first outing with her was to a club in Lubbock, not far from the Texas Tech University campus. She knew how to get us in even though we were only 19 and not the legal age. We danced with guys we didn't know and with each other. She got me turned on to Amaretto Sours. They really were quite yummy. I didn't get drunk … but I came close.

We went riding around with a group we didn't know from Texas Tech. They were going to take us back to their dorm, but I spoiled the party by refusing when I realized what was happening. Serena reluctantly took me back to Levelland. She was mad but she got over it. My roommate was out of town for the weekend so I could come in late and semi drunk without anyone else knowing it. I didn't tell Larry about this one till weeks later.

I went with Serena another time to the same club. This time I tried Pina Coladas. I've never liked beer because during my freshman year of high school I drank it hot with friends after running in a track meet. We drank it behind the school bus. Hot beer after a run on a hot day did me in FOREVER. But I soon found out that these wonderful sweet drinks were more my thing.

The third time I went out with Serena was my last time. Her boyfriend picked us up at our dorm and drove us to Lubbock to a country dance hall. It wasn't the usual college crowd, this was a much more mature group. I knew that I shouldn't have put myself in that situation. I had clear knowledge of right and wrong. This totally felt wrong as soon as I got in the car and realized her boyfriend had brought his dad along. I was tied up in knots on the inside. I didn't see a way out. The dad reminded me of my step dad and the way he looked at me made my skin crawl. I can honestly say that my Mom Melton's prayers must have been happening. Only by the grace and protection of God did I survive that evening. I drank that night but not near as much as Serena and the guys. She danced a lot with both of them and I kept to myself.

Her boyfriend was the only one that made a move on me when she was dancing with his dad. Thank you Lord that nothing major happened. I was so relieved when we got back to our dorms late that night. Partying with Serena had lost its charm. I guess I wasn't cut out to be a rebel without a cause after all. God really did have His hand of protection over me.

Surprise! Surprise!

Around noon the following morning, Serena and I walked to a fast food joint not far from our dorm. On our way, I got the surprise of my life. Larry pulled up next to us as we were walking down the street. He was mad. Just one look at both of us showed we had hangovers. He drove us the rest of the way and grilled me about where I had been. It was Valentine's Day weekend. He made the trip to surprise me. When he got to town Friday night and went to my dorm, they told him I wasn't in my room and didn't know where I was. He waited outside my dorm till late then spent the night in his brother's dorm room.

I knew I couldn't lie so I told him everything. He knew it was completely out of character for me, so he let Serena have it and demanded to know where her boyfriend worked. We made a trip over there. It was important to me for Larry to know that I didn't have sex with anyone. He was really and truly my one and only. I stayed in the pickup while Serena took Larry in and he talked to the unsuspecting, hungover guy. It was a really bad day for all of us.

Larry made sure that we all owned up to what we did that night. He was the only clear headed one even though his heart was broken. He felt like I had betrayed him. When Larry and Serena got back in the pickup with me, he was completely satisfied that nothing sexual had happened. His dislike towards Serena was evident. We dropped her off at the dorm and rode around talking, just the two of us. He slowly cooled off and I went back to my dorm to clean up for a date night. Being with Larry was so much more fun. I didn't have to drink to enjoy myself. He took me to a steakhouse in Lubbock and then we went back to his brother's dorm. I spent the night there totally happy in his arms. A lot happened that night. In fact, we NEVER forgot that night. Spending time with Larry for Valentine's weekend created a gift that would catapult us quickly into marriage and adulthood.

The Gift

A few weeks later I had a stomach flu I couldn't shake, it was awful. I love chocolate, but the box of Valentine chocolates was still uneaten. The only thing that got me awake in the mornings was the severe nausea that hit as soon as my eyes fluttered open. I had the darndest time getting to my 9:00 am classes. All I wanted to do was sleep. I was determined that I wasn't going to let college kick my butt again like nursing school had, so I dragged myself to each and every class. One friend was really concerned about me, and I talked her into taking me to Taco Villa for a bean burrito EVERY day. I would buy her one too to reward her for driving me. She suggested that I go see a doctor, she even offered to go with me. We went early one morning before classes. The receptionist handed me a cup and told me to pee in it and give to the nurse. I told her I'd only been nauseated for a couple of weeks. She had already diagnosed me … and she didn't even have a medical degree.

No Options

I did as I was told and came back to sit in the waiting room for what seemed like hours, but was actually minutes. My friend and I were the only two in the room. I was seriously hoping it was a bad case of the flu, it was the height of flu season. I wasn't an idiot. I knew the possibility … but I kept telling myself it was just the flu, just the flu … The nurse called me back and I went alone. I sat on that exam table with all the white in the room and felt enormous fear and anxiety. What was I going to do if my worst fear was confirmed?

The doctor walked in and I held my breath. He barely looked up from the chart in his hand as he read the results of my urine sample. That white room began to spin when he said the words, "You're pregnant." I couldn't breathe and I didn't. Quickly, without any emotion, he began to tell me what my options were.

"Options?" I thought … "Oh NO!"

I took a deep breath and said, "No, I do not have options." I lowered my head in shame. Fear rose in my belly as my mind raced to comprehend this moment.

An abortion was out of the question. I had been raised in the Baptist church. An abortion was NOT an option. I didn't know what I *was* going to, do but I did know what I *wasn't* going to do.

I paid my bill and walked past my friend. I needed out of there as fast as I could and I needed to breathe fresh air. An elephant was sitting on my chest and my heart was pounding so hard and so fast I was sure she could see it.

My friend knew what was going on though I didn't say a word. She took me back to my room and I skipped classes for the first time.

I cried till I felt dehydrated.

I didn't know what I was going to do, but I did know what I wasn't going to do.

The Proposal?!

Finally, around noon, I took a deep breath in, got my change together and walked to the end of the hall where there were two booths with pay phones. I knew Larry should be in the office for lunch, so I went into the booth, shut the door tightly and made the call. He was completely quiet as I explained the nausea, the visit to the doctor, and the diagnosis. That boy became a man that day and fully stepped into responsibility. I had always dreamed of a romantic marriage proposal … that was not to be. Instead I got, "Don't worry about doing this alone, we'll get married."

My dreams were shattered. This wasn't how it was supposed to go. In between sniffles, my answer was a simple, "Okay … " A sigh escaped—it came from so deep inside that as it escaped, I felt completely deflated.

"Wow," I thought ... I mean, I always knew we'd get married, but I just wanted Christie to finish school before we did.

"I'm pregnant ... " she said on the phone. She sounded so scared. I heard her say the words and my knees went weak.

At first I was even a little bit excited ... until I thought about having to tell our parents—hers and mine. I hung up with Christie, and the first person I told was my boss, Don. He was standing in the office right beside me when she called. He knew something was up.

"Christie is pregnant," I told him.

He had a cigarette in his mouth slowly puffing. He took it out, started laughing and said, "I always knew you two would get married ... it's about time!"

His laugh put me oddly at ease. For sure I didn't want it all to happen this way. I had dreamed of romantically proposing to her after I finished the house. I was planning to cook my signature dish, Cheeseburger Hamburger Helper with chopped up bell peppers and sliced tomatoes on top.

Some days when it was hard building the house, I'd think about the moment I would propose to Christie, it was for her and our future that I was building this house. Thinking about it was what kept me going. The plan had a snag now.

Dang Jonesie, you still owe me that "gourmet" dinner! Maybe for our fiftieth ...

Shockwaves

I made arrangements to ride home with my future sister in law that weekend, we shared the cost of gas. I wasn't very good company. I kept quiet and to myself, mainly because riding in the car made me super nauseated and I had a lot on my mind. She took me straight to where Larry was as soon as we got into town. I didn't tell her my secret. He grabbed my stuff out of the car and we rode around in his pickup talking about everything that had happened. I needed him so badly, my stomach was tied up in knots with fear, anxiety, and morning sickness that seemed to last all day. He was Mr. Calm, Cool and Collected. I didn't feel worthy of him.

Neither his parents nor mine knew I was in town. After a couple of hours of creating a plan and deciding what to say and how to say it, which by the way there is NO easy way, we got the nerve up to go to my house first.

It was dark outside, but still early enough to catch my mother and stepdad awake. They were surprised to see me and were concerned. Of course, I looked as nervous as a cat in a room full of rocking chairs. They were both seated in front of the TV. By the looks on our faces, they knew whatever we had to talk about must be important, so the TV was turned off. I blurted out, "I'm pregnant." Whew, what a relief to get those words out. They were stunned. Silent.

My brother had just turned four years old and in a few months, she was going to be a generation older. No doubt my mother was freaking out inside about becoming a grandmother. I couldn't really think about that right then. I was freaking out inside about becoming a mother.

They asked appropriate questions. Mother shed a few tears. Larry told them we were getting married the weekend after I finished my semester at college, which would be mid-May. The whole conversation didn't last long. I told them I would be back after we told Larry's parents the news. When we walked out of the house I took in a deep sigh of relief, I had survived!

His mother looked me eye-to-eye with a stern tone to her voice and asked, "Do you love him?"

"Yes, I do," I replied with confidence and that was that.

Larry said, "We are going to get married."

His mom looked straight at him and with the same stern voice said, "Yes. You are."

Nothing more needed to be said after that. It was settled. We drove around, making plans until we knew both of our parents would be sound asleep when we came home.

Tarnished Reputations

There were no congratulations or squeals of joy that we were getting married or that we were having a baby from either set of parents. Fear and anxiety had such a grip on me that even I had a hard time feeling any excitement. "What were people going to say?" I wondered. Our reputations and our parents' reputations were now tarnished. Everyone kept quiet about the reason we were getting married in 6 weeks. Everyone knew, of course, but nice people—nice Baptist people—didn't talk about these things. There was a lot to do.

Planning the Wedding

The next day my mother told me that they would pay for a small, informal wedding. They had gotten an income tax return check from the IRS. I was overwhelmed at her sacrifice.

Larry asked his dad to be his best man and two of his brothers to be his groomsmen, his youngest brother would be an usher. My dear friend, Pam, was my maid of honor and my two sisters my bridesmaids

Bare Necessities

We went to Amarillo, a 2-hour drive, to pick out our rings. We purchased them at Service Merchandise for less than $300 total for both his and mine. It was all we could afford and so dear to both of us. Larry had finished the house and was beginning to furnish it, most everything he had was second hand, but he wanted to buy a new bed. I'm laughing because what we chose isn't even in style anymore! We bought a King size waterbed. It was as beautiful to us as our rings. He put his ring and my wedding band away. There was no special ceremony of giving me my engagement ring. He simply handed the ring to me and I put it on.

The excitement of getting married was beginning to push out more of the fear and anxiety. I really did love Larry and I couldn't imagine my life without him. How it came about cast a shadow, but the sun was starting to shine through. I was going to be with Larry happily ever after.

Finishing What I Started

I went back to school and worked hard at keeping my grades up. There were only two people I told I was pregnant. I was very proud of my dainty ring and showed it off, excitedly telling my college friends that I was getting married.

Planning the wedding was a challenge. I had ideas and my mother had ideas. Because I wasn't home, she made the decisions. Looking back now I realize that she knew her budget and was working within her parameters. I made the trip home a couple of times, and between my mother and Larry's mother it all came together.

"How am I going to be able to provide for Christie and a baby?" was the focus of my thoughts. I wasn't as worried about the whole situation as she was, and I knew we were meant for each other. I wasn't real close to God, like I am now. I knew He loved me even though I had sinned by having sex before marriage. I just couldn't keep my hands off of her. Yet ... someway, somehow I knew I would find a way to provide and our love would grow. I planned all along to grow old with this girl.

Outpouring of Community Love

A couple of weekends before the wedding we had our bridal shower. There were a dozen hostesses. One of Larry's classmate's moms hosted our shower at her ranch house, she was a prominent lady of the community. I was overwhelmed by the outpouring of gifts and love they all showed to us. The house was filled to overflowing with gifts and with ladies. Larry sat next to me and helped open the gifts. It took both of us well over two hours to unwrap everything, I actually got really tired. Who knew a person could get such a workout from opening gifts?

I knew that their niceness was mainly because of their love for Larry, but it was sweet that they accepted me even though I was pregnant. By this time, most of them knew, but none of them talked about it in front of us. It was a small town. In small towns news travels fast. They had already accepted me as one of their own. I did not understand this kind of love and I didn't know how to accept it. I felt so undeserving.

I Did It

Sunday came and I went back to college for my final push to finish out the semester. I took my exams and passed with flying colors. I had experienced a semester of college, living in the dorm. It was a unique experience that I will treasure. Circumstances had changed. A new path had emerged. I found I was ready to move on to the next chapter in my life—being a wife and a mother.

I did not understand this kind of love and I didn't know how to accept it. I felt so undeserving.

CHAPTER EIGHT

New Beginnings—
The Vow

"*For this cause shall a man leave his father and mother, and shall cleave to his wife; and the two shall become one flesh: so that they are no more two, but one flesh. What therefore God hath joined together, let no man put asunder.*"

MARK 10:7-9, ASV

My Favorite Baptist Preacher

We chose Larry's cousin John to officiate our vows. He was much older than us and a Baptist preacher. Cousin John, however, was NOT the typical preacher. He looked like Burt Reynolds and had a quirky sense of humor.

He asked to meet me by myself to get to know me. I only knew of him, we had never met. I was worried about judgement and condemnation for getting pregnant out of marriage, but the opposite happened. I had never sat across the table with a preacher before.

We met for lunch at Dairy Queen. In Texas, that's comfort food and I chose it because it was familiar and it put me at ease. Cousin John was light hearted and funny, with a mischievous twinkle in his eye. I laughed a lot. I liked him instantly. His personality was not stern or austere or made me feel like God was about to pounce because of my mistakes. He can bless the socks off people with his knowledge of the scriptures and the joy that flows out of him. To this day, he is still one of my favorite preachers.

Two Promises

Later that day he met with Larry and I together. He told Larry that he approved of me with a chuckle in his voice and then made us promise two things: One, to never go to bed angry with each other, and two, never sleep apart. Those were two promises we had no idea would be so tough to keep. Over the next few years there were many heated disagreements that went well into the early morning hours before they were resolved. There were also nights I'd be so mad at that man of mine that I would grab my pillow and a blanket to sleep in the living room on the couch. I'd get all settled in and hear Larry getting settled in with his pillow and a blanket on the floor next to me. He'd simply say, "We made a promise to never sleep apart." I'd smile in the dark, my quick temper deflating and mellowing me out with his simple acts of love and commitment.

Details Came Together

I originally wanted to have an outdoor wedding. Larry's parents had a nice backyard until his dad sprayed ground kill on the grass, thinking it was weed killer. Their lush green backyard turned to dirt for a full year.

The First Baptist Church was available. I didn't feel worthy of being married in the church, but that's what happened. God made sure of it, that stinker. Purple was my favorite color, and there were hints of deep purple, lavender, and lilac here and there. I borrowed a wedding dress from Dolores, a sweet friend of my mother's, and a classy hat with veil from my cousin Jana.

The Wedding

I slept on the couch at my parent's house the night before the wedding. Mother gave my bed to company. I was super nauseated and my allergies were so bad that I constantly had a tickle in my throat and coughed a lot. The dress hid any barely noticeable changes happening to my body. A relief.

My brother was our ring bearer … and I'm still waiting for an opportunity to get him back for stealing the show. He was 3 years old and so stinking cute as he walked down the aisle with my youngest cousin. She was a proper young lady, but my brother would visit with people as he walked down the aisle. During the ceremony, he had to be physically removed off the stage for pretending to drive the ring bearer pillow, while making tractor noises while going back and forth across the front of the church. He had everyone laughing. Larry's dad held the wedding rings. We have it all on video …

> I will never forget the day I took Christie's hand and vowed in my heart that I would never let go of it, no matter what. When I placed the ring on her finger I was fully aware it would be forever and I didn't want anything less. When I saw her coming down the aisle, it was if no one else was in the church. I locked eyes with her and realized she was all mine. My cousin John leaned over to me and whispered, "She's beautiful."

> I totally agreed, she was the most beautiful thing I had ever seen.

I personally believe that God placed in Larry a special love for me. He had to rely heavily on God to help him as he held me close through some dark times over the years. God gave him strength often when he had none on his own. Many times I heard him whisper, "Lord, help me" and he meant it!

The guys worked hard on "decorating" Larry's pickup. They wired the horn to honk every time the brakes were used. Attached to the front grill of the pickup was the largest pair of men's Fruit of the Loom underwear anybody had ever seen. Someone created a brown streak down the crack of it and mounted it rear end facing. I don't know what some of you had to endure, but all of this was horrifying to me! We had so much rice thrown at us that we left a trail wherever we went. Just when we thought we had cleaned the last bit out, we would randomly find a grain of rice in odd places. That pickup probably still had rice when we traded it in for a family car the next year!

The Overnight Honeymoon

On our way to our honeymoon destination, which was a Lodge at a lake in Oklahoma, the pickup "farted and died." That's what Larry referred to it as. What actually happened was that it backfired and quit working. We managed to roll to the side of the road. We were within 30 minutes of our destination and broke down on the side of a county road that looked like it was barely used in the middle of nowhere. A kind farmer took mercy on us and stopped to help. There was no mistaking we were newlyweds on our way to our honeymoon. We got in with him, he took us to his home where he picked up his wife and they dropped us off at the lodge. Larry wrote down their address and we sent them a thank you note a couple of weeks later.

We called Larry's dad the next morning, and he brought some parts with him. He picked us up and the two of them spent the afternoon in the hot sun repairing the pickup, then we went home. There was only enough money to spare for a one-night honeymoon. We had a new house, that was far more important to us than a grand honeymoon ... that WAS our luxury resort.

Settling in To Married Life

Larry worked a lot of long hours with his full-time job and his part time work. I got a job at the local grocery store as a cashier. I would practice my cooking skills after I got home from work. That poor man certainly didn't marry me for my cooking. I know I mentioned earlier that I wasn't a good cook, but ya'll I was REALLY bad. I did

NOT know how to use all the awesome kitchen items we received as gifts.

In the beginning, all I knew how to make was hot dogs and spaghetti so we alternated between the two until Larry's mom was asking him how things were going. He simply told her what our two meals mainly consisted of. She said to me, "He must really love you, he hasn't eaten wienies since he won the Boy Scout hot dog eating contest when he was younger and threw them all up." I looked at Larry and asked him if that was true. He blushed and laughed. I got those cookbooks out and was determined I was going to feed him things he liked.

Feeling Inferior

Tammy was my sister-in-law, married to Larry's older brother, Bobby. She was a good Christian girl, raised in a neighboring community with parents that were highly regarded. I couldn't hold a candle to how good she was. Larry's other brother, Ronny was engaged to Sherri and they were to be married the next year. Sherri was Homecoming Queen and Head Cheerleader the year we graduated. Sherri and Tammy were everything Larry's mother wanted for her sons. I needed A LOT of work. I was always feeling like I fell short of everyone's expectations.

CHAPTER NINE

Haley ... Unconditional Love

———— ❧ ————

"Love is patient, love is kind and is not jealous; love does not brag and is not arrogant, does not act unbecomingly; it does not seek its own, is not provoked, does not take into account a wrong suffered, does not rejoice in unrighteousness, but rejoices with the truth; bears all things, believes all things, hopes all things, endures all things. Loves never fails."

1 CORINTHIANS 13:4-8A, NASB

Mine Wasn't the First Grandchild

A few days after we got married, my younger sister who had confided with me about the sexual abuse while I was living with my Mom Melton dropped a bombshell. She told my mother that she was almost five months pregnant. My mother hit the roof. I'll admit, that was a lot to take in. Both of us had gotten pregnant before marriage.

She was not quite 16 years old. She wasn't in love with the father of her baby, and there would be no wedding bells. My mother must have felt like she had failed parenting. Growing up she never talked about sex with us. We had both read the book she provided on the subject, and she also relied on the fact that she took us to church every time the doors opened. Somehow, neither of those things changed the outcome.

Normal Pregnancy

My "baby" doctor was a general physician several people used as an OB. His office was in a town about an hour away.

The pregnancy went well. I was a healthy 19-year old girl and experienced no complications.

Larry and I attended Lamaze classes. It was important to me to have a natural birth without medications for pain.

We never had a sonogram, we couldn't afford one.

Names were picked out for either a boy or a girl. If it was a boy, Larry wanted to name him George Jones after the Country and Western singer ... I said NO! We honestly didn't care what sex our baby was.

For my twentieth birthday Larry bought the car seat/infant carrier I had picked out.

There were no pre-labor pains or false alarms, and I was three days past our due date when I went into labor.

The Delivery

My sister's new baby girl had made her way into the world just three weeks earlier, and my mother had her hands full caring for them. So when my contractions began, instead of heading to my mom's we went to Larry's parents.

Larry's mom felt how hard my tummy was and immediately began putting rollers in her hair—she wanted to look good for her first grand baby. When she was all dolled up they followed us to the hospital an hour away.

They hooked me up to a monitor that measured the contractions. Larry's dad kept an eye on the monitor and would call out the strong contractions like a play-by-play radio announcer for a sporting event.

My water had to be broken. There wasn't a lot of fluid and they were concerned, but I didn't have any idea what that might mean. Immediately the baby began to come. The doctor arrived just in time for me to push and our 6 pound, 4 ounce baby girl entered our world.

She had a headful of dark brown hair like her daddy's and his round face. She was perfect.

I had done it all without any pain meds and when I saw that beautiful angelic face, it was worth it all. The pain of laboring for 6 hours was completely replaced with joy and love that I had never felt before, it was deep.

She didn't cry much and her reactions were a bit sluggish, but no one seemed concerned. Larry's parents were elated when they met their first grandchild.

We named her Haley Ann.

Halley's Comet was a much talked about phenomenon at that time, and I loved the name Haley. Larry's mother's name was Ann, and it was important to us for our first child to share names with her Granny. His parents were now known as Granny and PawPaw and very proud of it.

Later, Granny told us that her grandfather was named Halley after the comet coming by in 1910. It makes a showing about every 75-76 years. In a few days, this same comet was going to shoot around the earth again, and I loved that there was this special connection with our baby's great, great grandfather.

My Perfect Baby ... So I Thought

I had planned to breastfeed, but Haley had no interest whatsoever. She wanted to sleep more than eat. Getting her to take a bottle was a struggle. I thought she was the perfect baby, and I dressed her like a baby doll every day. She had Nestle's Baby Hair Lotion rubbed on her scalp daily with a little tiny matching ribbon tied in a bow that I used clear Karo syrup to attach a clump of hair on her tiny head. Granny had meticulously made her a tiny ribbon bow in every color imaginable.

She had also sewed curtains and baby blankets, and Haley's nursery was all Care Bears.

Even though she wasn't planned, this baby girl was deeply adored,

Warning Signs

Many nights during her first weeks of life, I set an alarm to feed our infant baby girl. She was quickly losing weight, and she required a special soy based formula that was very expensive and hard to find. Larry's mom knew something was not right, so she insisted on going to Haley's six-week checkup with me. She had some questions for the doctor. I was totally oblivious, what I saw was a perfect baby.

After hearing her concerns, our doctor decided to have Haley seen by a developmental pediatrician in Amarillo.

A week later Larry took off from work and we took our adorable, innocent child to the first of oh so many specialists to come.

The older female doctor knew something wasn't right. She sent us to the hospital for a CT scan that day. For three more precious days, we were a "normal" family.

The Call and Home Alone

I was home alone when the country doctor called me with the results of Haley's CT scan. I was numb, no tears as he casually told me that our precious baby was missing part of her brain and would be profoundly retarded. The ocean of tears would come later. Multiple questions were imploding in my fully intact brain.

Missing? Where was it? What happened? Retarded? What had I done wrong? Neither of us had ever done drugs and definitely no alcohol during pregnancy. I had a normal pregnancy, I had taken no medications during child birth. We had gone through Lamaze classes, I gave birth completely naturally. What could possibly have caused this? Then it hit me! This was God punishing us for having sex before marriage. We were both virgins when we met and fell in love ... but I was 3 months pregnant when I got married—*had to* get married.

My own mind couldn't take in any more information, the doctor must have sensed it on the other end of the phone. He asked me if anyone was home with me, and I quickly told him no. Next he asked me to call my husband and notify close family members. He stated that I didn't need to be home alone with this news.

He had me schedule an appointment for the next day so he could further discuss the results of the CT scan with Larry and me. He said he had options to discuss with us.

"Options?" I thought, "How do you fix a brain part that is missing?"

Forever Changed

I sat in total silence looking at my beautiful baby girl who was sleeping peacefully in the antique white bassinet beside me. Just moments before she looked like a normal baby.

From that day forth there was nothing "normal" in our lives.

I mustered up the strength to call Larry at work. When he came to the phone, he knew by my voice that something was wrong. He immediately came home. He walked through the door and the ocean of tears started for both of us. It came in waves.

The Bible says, "You keep track of all my sorrows. You have collected all my tears in your bottle. You have recorded each one in your book" (Psalm 56:8, NLT).

In Heaven there is a MIGHTY BIG bottle and a HEFTY book imprinted with my name.

"I don't want to believe this," Larry said, "this cannot be true." Just like me, Larry was in denial that anything wrong with our beloved daughter could not be fixed. We both felt that surely there was something that could be done to fix it.

Haley needed diapers, so we went to the grocery store together. I remember pushing a shopping cart down the aisle as if it was a normal day, but feeling totally lifeless and numb inside. As a child, I had learned to survive abuse without anyone knowing. I reactivated the survival skill so that no one else knew how different I was from them.

I didn't personally know anyone with a child with no mid brain that was profoundly retarded.

Everyone in the store I saw was normal, I was far from it.

Suffocating

We went to that appointment heavy hearted with the weight of the world sitting on our shoulders. I couldn't breathe. I felt like I was going to suffocate. While holding sweet Haley in my arms, that doctor told us she would never walk or talk, she would be primarily non-responsive due to what all was missing in her brain.

He told us that she would require lots of care and that there was a service center in Amarillo that we could contact that would put us in touch with specialists.

He wasn't prepared to keep us on as patients. We would need to find a pediatrician.

We left that appointment totally hopeless.

Reactions

When I mustered the nerve to tell my mother, she was no comfort. She freaked out when I told her about Haley.

She went to the Christian Bookstore and bought me a book about how to care for a brain injured child. I never read that book, but I knew it was my mother's way of doing her best to help. Whenever she didn't have the answer or know what to do she bought a book, the author was her professional or teacher.

When I was young I returned from a very enlightening slumber party at a friend's house and asked my mother about sex. She went out straight away and bought me a book that explained the anatomy of men and women and how babies are conceived. I read that book cover to cover several times over, and so did my sisters.

Granny and PawPaw did all they could do. I know Granny hated that her gut feelings were right.

No one on either side of our families had ever had this problem.

I only knew about my mother's side, she didn't want me to know anything about my biological dad. That was a secret she would take to her grave. His name on my birth certificate was all I knew about him.

I became very angry at God. How could He be so mean and cruel to punish us and our daughter? We were the ones that made the choice to have sex before marriage. Haley was completely innocent, but yet the product of our sin and the result was cursing us by cursing her. I totally believed with every cell in my body that I was being punished by a very cruel God. My tunnel was dark, there was no light!

Doing What It Takes

Region 16 Service Center came to our home monthly. We had a great caseworker, Judith, who spoke truth to me. She told me I had to be Haley's voice and stand up for her. I couldn't be mousey and whiney. I needed to be tough and do whatever it took to help my child.

My full-time job became Haley. I took her to every therapist and specialist I heard of.

Larry was working hard to keep us from going bankrupt.

Our whole town showed deep compassion towards us.

Lots of Expenses

Larry was offered lots of part time jobs to keep us out of the red. We had a large Mason jar in our kitchen that we kept our gas and food money in. There were times we searched for coins to go buy a loaf of bread or gallon of milk. We whooped and hollered when we found a quarter. Every penny was valued.

Because of Haley's medical condition, we qualified for government help. I went to the Social Security office many times before we started getting a monthly check to help with her medical expenses. They offered us food stamps, but we both declined that. We had too much pride. It was one thing to get a check in the mail that was deposited in an account and another to stand in line at the grocery store where everyone saw that a person was poor by using food stamps.

I couldn't work to make enough money to hire someone to take care of all of Haley's needs and make a profit. Larry was the one that worked the long, tough hours.

I had my own long, tough hours taking care of all the doctor and therapy appointments.

Haley was taken to every kind of therapy, doctor, and specialist imaginable.

Special toys and equipment were either bought or made.

This child was our world.

She looked like a little Cabbage Patch baby; round faced with beautiful, thick, dark brown hair—like her daddy's—and a giggle that caused everyone around her to chuckle.

She responded to people and she responded to therapy.

We only resorted to medications on occasion, when necessary, for short increments.

There was a strength that rose up in me. I was determined this child WAS going to walk and talk and feed herself ... in her own timing, she did!

Nothing came easy for her or for any of us.

Haley has taught me unconditional love in the deepest and purest sense. I had to learn how to step into her world in order to bring her into our world. Her world is a simpler, more fun, and far less complicated place. To be honest, I prefer her world at times.

This child was going to walk and talk and feed herself!

Love

God used Haley to teach me about love. I didn't know I had that much love in me for a little human being. You add on all the difficulties and my natural compassion exploded.

I feared God, I didn't love Him. I cried out to Him for help for her benefit, I didn't feel I deserved any.

I felt like I was the reason she was born the way she was. Larry and I both worked super hard to right our wrong. We felt like we were being punished.

People would tell us that God gave her to us because we were special, He knew we could handle it.

Special wasn't what we felt …

CHAPTER TEN

Loss and Grief at Twenty-One

"The Lord is near to the brokenhearted and saves those who are crushed in spirit."

PSALMS 34:18, NASB

Secrets

About the time I felt like I could deal with everything, I got another blow. My mother called and wanted me to come see her. We had grown apart for two reasons, both were caused by deep hurts. The first one had to do with Haley. There was a genetic specialist working with us to help determine the cause of Haley's abnormalities, and she needed detailed information about Larry's family and my family. His mom and dad freely gave whatever information they had. Although my mother would tell me anything I wanted to know about her side of the family, she blew up and refused to give ANY information about my biological father or his family. I couldn't understand why she wouldn't give me the information I desperately needed for Haley. Without full information about both sides of our family, they couldn't determine a cause so we were told it could have been environmental and gave us a 25% chance of it happening again. That was strong enough odds for me. Not knowing if what happened to Haley would happen again, we were afraid to have any more children. I went on birth control.

The second reason we had grown apart was because of her husband. My mother had come down hard on my sister, and in the heat of an argument called her a slut for being sexually active and getting pregnant. My sister broke and told her about the sexual abuse she had endured for years from our stepdad. Mother came to my house banging on the door. I let her in and she furiously demanded answers. I told her everything my sister had told her was true, and what he had tried to do to me when I was 16.

She left my house and went to the Sheriff's office, telling them about the accusations. I don't know for sure what happened when she got home and confronted her husband of 15 years, but the next day she went back to the Sheriff's office and told them it was all a lie. They told her a caseworker from Child Protective Services had already been assigned the case and that they would be investigating the allegations of sexual abuse and would be contacting us for our testimonies.

Manipulation

Mother came to my house and sat down in a chair, almost lifeless, no ranting and raving. I didn't know what to make of it. She told me that I couldn't tell a soul about the abuse, we had to keep it all a secret. Her husband had threatened to commit suicide if she didn't recant her story. He had promised to get counseling and to pay for counseling for my sister who was just 16 years old and still in their home. She told me I would be fine, I had Larry. I told her Larry already knew about it all.

While we were talking, we heard a car pull up in my driveway. I didn't recognize the car and didn't know the woman driving it. I looked through the little window in the door. My mother locked the front door, grabbed my hand, and pulled me into Haley's room which was closest to the driveway. Haley was sound asleep in her baby crib. She whispered that I had to remain quiet, and if I testified against her husband his suicide would be my fault. Could I live with the guilt of his death because I exposed him? He was promising to never do it again and to seek help. She assured me that my silence would be the best for my family.

The woman stood at my front door and rang the doorbell several times. My mother's vehicle and mine were completely visible. It seemed like forever before she gave up and left. Mother hurried out the door in case she went to her house to question my sister. I felt horrible and dirty all over again like I did as a child, but this time my mother knew and she chose to protect him over us. I lost a lot of respect for her that day. I hated that she had a chance to right a wrong and wouldn't. She was just as guilty as he was, she knew the truth and didn't do anything.

Yes, I was free to go to the Sheriff's office and tell them the truth, but I had my own battle for survival going on with Haley's health issues. I deeply wanted my mother to fight for us. I didn't have it in me to fight two battles at once. I also didn't want the whole town to know how dirty our lives were. Though I hadn't done anything wrong, I still felt shame.

That caseworker came again the next day. I watched her through a tiny sliver through the mini blinds in Haley's room. My heart ached to tell the truth, but I hoped mother was right that he would get professional help—the Lord knows he desperately needed it. What I didn't know at the time was that if they had followed through with counseling, which they didn't, an investigation would have been started because a counselor has to report abuse.

I think my stepdad knew this too, it was just a ploy to get mother to lie for him ... manipulation and control. I didn't have much to do with my family after that. It was hard pretending that nothing had happened.

Tired of Life

So when my mother called several months later, wanting just me to come over to talk to her, I knew something was up. Larry watched Haley for me.

When I arrived, my sisters were quiet in other rooms. The house had a gloomy feel to it. Mother was in her room, propped up with pillows lying in bed even though it was late afternoon. She didn't look good. She had no makeup on. She patted the bed beside her for me to sit down. I chose to stand with my arms crossed. She told me that she had been to the doctor earlier in the week because her side hurt a lot. He thought it was pleurisy, but ordered an x-ray to make sure. There was a big shadow across her liver so she had a biopsy done. The results were that she had cancer and she was in the end stages. She didn't have long to live. I went to her and she held me and we cried together for a long time. She had a roll of toilet paper sitting beside her that we both used to wipe away the snot and tears, it was the really ugly kind of crying.

"Gosh Lord," I thought, "How big is that bottle that holds our tears? That's one big book You have, recording every tear ..."

After we both settled and we had the energy to talk, she told me she was tired of living and was really ready to die. She knew she would go to heaven, her only concerns were leaving her children. She wanted to make sure we were all taken care of. She was less worried about me, because I had Larry. She thought the world of Larry. When I asked her how long she had to live, she told me they had given her 6 months. She asked me to come to her if there was anything I had questions about from my childhood. I immediately asked her to tell me about my biological father. She answered, "I'll tell you anything you want to know except that," and that was the end of that conversation. She took all that she knew and didn't want me to know with her to the grave.

Dealing with Death at 21

The days ahead were tough. Mother wanted to die at home not in a hospital. Within days of her biopsy her skin began to turn yellow: jaundice was the medical term. All of this happened within the week before Easter. At church, I went to the same Sunday School class that she attended so it was full of ladies who knew us both quite well. My mother was already too ill to attend church. When I walked in that room, there were quiet conversations going on about the news of my mother. When they all realized I had walked in, the room fell silent and everyone looked away. No hugs, no comfort.

It was the last time I attended that class with those women.

The ladies of the church were good at keeping meals supplied for my mother and siblings. The pastor made frequent visits.

Mother was in and out of the hospital several times to get her pain regulated and due to complications of the cancer. Finally, she refused any treatment and wanted only Hospice. My stepdad's mother came to take care of her, that's the only person he would allow. My mother was on high doses of morphine and other pain killers, sometimes she talked randomly. I think he was afraid of what might slip through her lips about him. He continued to work, while his mother took care of the daily needs and a Hospice nurse made periodic home visits to monitor her pain level and adjust her meds.

My mother's family members were allowed to come for short visits, but not stay to care for her.

Mother was surrounded by her children and those that deeply loved her when she took her last breath on this side of heaven. It was in the wee hours of the night, 101 days from her diagnosis, on July 25, 1987. I was 21. My sister had just graduated, my youngest sister would be a senior in high school, my brother had just turned 5 and would start school the following fall as a kindergartner. She was 41 years old.

I witnessed a peace come across her whole body, evident in the relaxing of her face almost into a smile.

It was a long time before the Justice of the Peace came and pronounced her dead and took her body to the funeral home. While we waited, my sister left the room and returned with four sealed envelopes with each of mine and my sibling's names written by my mother. One for each of her beloved children. My sister had been given strict instructions not to give them to us till after she died. Mother wanted us to be comforted when the time came. She loved us all dearly. I have never read my sibling's letters but this is what mine said:

My Sweet Christie

Words are so hard at times like these. I have nothing to leave you as far as material things, but I hope I left you all my love and I want you to share it with Haley and Larry, they both are special to me. I hope all that we have been through that you'll remember the good times we've had, that's all that is important in life sweetheart. Forget hurts, forget hate and just love life, it's so precious and can be taken so quickly. So as my legacy I leave you the love in the world and you will be the richest person on earth, because that's all it really takes to live here.

I would like to write you a novel but this has been the hardest to write. Big lumps keep getting in the way. Take good care of our sweet Larry and Haley and whoever else may come along later. I think you have a good chance for giving Larry a boy. I'll have good connections and see to it.

Christie, I love you. You were my first born and so special to me. I was new at motherhood and made lots of mistakes, but you were never a mistake. I always wanted you and loved you with all my heart. I love you.

Larry, you are very special, you're a good husband and a good daddy. I always loved you from the start. I knew you would be a good son-in-law. Take care of my Christie, she'll need you and take special care of Haley she is special in my heart too, I'll always be with you two in your hearts. I love you.

Your mother,

Judy

I sat on the front porch with the porch light on reading this letter after she passed while we waited for the JP. Larry sat beside me and held me as I cried. He looked up and saw a shooting star pass overhead, I got a glimpse of it.

There she goes. Judy has suffered from the time she turned jaundiced. She wasn't fighting it, she was ready to go. I think the Lord granted her heart's desire to go quickly. I honestly believe that shooting star was a sign to us, I'll always believe that.

Larry held me close as he spoke these words. I know it tore him up to see me hurting. He couldn't imagine losing his mom at such a young age, she was only 41, just a few years older than his own mom. My mother's passing made him want to spend more time with his mom and give her a big hug. Life is short.

Gone at 41

Mother had planned her funeral in advance, early after her diagnosis. She had the funeral director and the pastor come visit with her while we were out of the house and talk it all through. Her husband had not paid the renewal for her life insurance policy, and she knew there was very little money to bury her. She picked out the simplest casket. It was important to her that "Jesus Loves Me" was sung at her funeral for my 5-year-old brother. She was buried 5 hours away in an isolated country cemetery where my stepdad's family was buried. Her family is buried in Lubbock. I never asked her why she picked that spot. It never made sense to me. It was years before a headstone was placed at her grave. I don't visit her grave very often. When we visited once we encountered a huge snake that chased us … seriously! When I do go to her grave, it's usually in the dead of winter.

When her body was taken, we went home. I sat in a chair on our back porch looking up at the stars thinking, "I will never laugh again." There was no joy left in me, only deep sorrow. When I did finally go to bed I had a dream. In that dream, I relived my mother taking her last breath. This time I saw Jesus reach His hand down and take hers. She smiled at Him and saw her daddy standing next to Jesus. He told her, "it's time to come home Judy," and she left us. Her next breath was in heaven, pain free, burden free and fully loved. The dream gave me the peace and comfort I needed to get through the next few days.

Life Goes on

The days that followed were hard. My younger sister, her baby, my brother, and our stepdad moved to the Abilene area to live with his mother. She enrolled in college classes, having graduated high school. I'm grateful that mother got to see her walk the stage to get her diploma before she died. I was deeply concerned about my sister and her baby leaving with him, but there was nothing I could do about the situation. God blessed me with my youngest sister coming to live with us. She was starting her senior year of high school and I loved having my baby sister with me. It really is true that life goes on. We needed each other. Her biological dad was my stepdad. She hadn't endured any abuse. He sent her money and she had a part time job at the courthouse to cover all her expenses. She was fun to be around and had a great sense of humor. She was a ray of sunshine. Her classes were half a day, then she came home for lunch and worked in the afternoons till 5:00.

My Mother's Line

I used one of the lines my mother used on me growing up one day when I had a feeling she was up to something. I said, "I know what you did last night." She blurted out that it wasn't her idea to go to that party. She came clean about the whole night, giving every detail.

"How did you know?" she asked me.

I told her, "It's a small town, you can't get away with anything." It was a very long time before I told her I only had a hunch, I really didn't know.

Hmmm ... how many times did my mother get information out of me using that same tactic?

Deeply Concerned

My stepdad started dating a woman with two young girls. A few years earlier, she had become a friend of my mother's. She was recently widowed and showed him much sympathy. They decided to get married right away. She needed a father figure for her children, and he needed a mother for my brother. Their wedding was exactly 4 months after my mother's death. I had no ill feelings towards her, I was deeply concerned because she had two young girls elementary age. I didn't want them to experience what my sister and I had gone through.

All I could do was pray for them. I had no fight in me. I can't express enough how much of a full-time job taking care of Haley was both physically and emotionally. We had doctor appointments and therapies out the wazoo. I also knew that if I caused any trouble, he would take my baby sister away from me. I treasured that ray of sunshine in my life, so I kept silent.

CHAPTER ELEVEN

Everybody Left

"The Lord Himself goes before you and will be with you; He will never leave you nor forsake you. Do not be afraid; do not be discouraged."

DEUTERONOMY 31:8, NIV

Little Sis Married and Gone

Little Sis met the love of her life while she was living with us. At first I wasn't too crazy about him, he drank a lot and had a reputation for driving drunk. He had been married for a very short time and was a couple of years older than her. He was a lot more experienced with life, and I wanted her to stay innocent, but she was in love. As I began to see him through her eyes he grew on me. He came from a well-respected family, with a mom and dad I liked a lot.

The summer of 1988 held a lot of hard changes for Larry and me. It had been one year since mother had died, Little Sis had graduated from high school and gotten married. She got married at the church in the town where her dad lived. There was no big wedding, just a small ceremony. I didn't get to go, it was held at the spur of the moment.

She married into a family that nurtured her well. His mom is as great a cook and housekeeper as my mother-in-law, and I feel like God blessed us with strong maternal women to help continue raising us.

They are still together. Larry and I grew very fond of our brother-in-law, he has been a good husband and father over the years. They have two children and now are grandparents.

Larry's Parents

I need to describe Granny, Larry's mother, to you. She has THE most beautiful white hair, it prematurely starting turning white when she was in her teen years. This woman is stout at a tinge over 5 feet tall. Everyone that meets her falls in love with her. She's a great people person, but don't ever cross her, she's fierce. I've rarely been on her fierce side, thank you Jesus. She has been above and beyond patient with me over the years and I have a great deal of respect for her. Don't get me wrong, we've gone head to head over some issues, but we both get over them fairly quickly.

PawPaw is the genius in my eyes. He's NOT a people person, in fact he is a grizzly bear to most of us, but a teddy bear with his grandchildren. He is gifted in painting, building, and technology.

If Larry didn't know what to do we always knew PawPaw would know.

The Big Move

When we had been married for three years, Larry's parents moved to Oklahoma City. Granny and PawPaw had raised their last son.

David was accepted to attend college at Oklahoma University, and Granny and PawPaw had already decided to take a job in Oklahoma City which would give PawPaw more benefits to be able to retire early. Granny got a great job at a bank and quickly moved up to running one of their branches.

They sold their house to the recently hired school principal and moved as soon as David graduated. All of their boys had been raised in that house, but they were ready for a new chapter. I can't begin to understand how hard of a move that was for them, but it was a smart move.

They were leaving. Our support system was GONE. They wouldn't be there to help us out with Haley any longer. We were devastated. We had come to rely on them a great deal and so loved having them as part of our lives.

Looking at the Bright Side

I will say there were many perks to them living in OKC, which was only about 2.5 hours away. We had a place to go out of town and visit without it costing us an arm and a leg. They bought a huge, four bedroom newly built home with three bathrooms, two living areas and two dining areas, it was Granny's dream house. The yard was little, that was PawPaw's dream yard. He put in a goldfish pond and deck which took up a third of the back yard. He could mow, weed eat, and edge in just a few minutes. The rest of his evenings were spent snoozing in his recliner. They appeared to flourish being on their own in the big city.

Holidays were fun when all of us would meet up at their house. The families were growing. Each of us had our own room. Bobby and Tammy had two children, Jordan and Alisha. We had Haley. Ronny and Sherri had married two years earlier and now had baby Tracy. David was still single, he got the couch in the living room.

Larry and I grew up even faster with them in OKC. We were completely on our own and it was good for us. We were more in love than ever and being alone just caused us to draw closer together.

Larry's Granny Goodwin and Great Grandpa Sears

Even though Haley didn't come with an instruction manual, we were surviving and she was thriving. We took on the responsibility of checking in on Larry's grandmother, Granny Goodwin, who was in the nursing home just a few blocks from our house. She had a lot of Indian in her, which gave her big beautiful brown eyes and high cheekbones. Her features were petite. She was prim and proper, but due to dementia could cuss us out like a sailor when she wasn't getting her way. Granny Goodwin was a brittle diabetic. She could have an extremely low or extremely high blood sugar reading without any known cause. She was sneaky too, so perhaps on occasion she ate something that none of us knew about. I remember walking into her room to check on her and she was ripping curtains off the window and throwing everything in the room around. I was completely shocked. Every time I had seen her before she was sweet as molasses. Alzheimers and Diabetes are hard diseases on individuals and on families.

Christie was right, all the years growing up I knew Granny Goodwin as a prim and proper lady and the best cook ever. She worked hard as a waitress in Shamrock, TX at the Maverick Restaurant on Route 66. It was a popular destination in its time. She took care of her Indian daddy who lived with her for years. She would take us boys with her to Anadarko, Oklahoma to the Indian Pow Wow. We would drop Great Grandpa off to visit with his Indian buddies. We went to the parade and kid friendly family attractions. That evening before dark we would pick Great Grandpa up.

On our way home we stopped in Texola, because Shamrock was located in Wheeler County which was a dry county and didn't allow alcohol sales. Granny would pull up to the liquor store, Grandpa would slowly walk in, a few minutes later he came out carrying a brown paper sack with one large bottle of whiskey that had to last him till next year's Indian Pow Wow. He would turn around to sit into the car. Hidden in his back pockets was two more flat bottles of whiskey. Granny knew but never let him know that she knew.

That little prim and proper lady could put us in our place. She never yelled, never spanked us, but if we got rowdy she would line all four of us boys across her couch and make us sit on our hands for what seemed like forever. Our entertainment while sitting on our hands was watching Great Grandpa Sears yell at wrestlers on the large wooden console TV.

Watching Granny Goodwin deteriorate was hard. She eventually had to have one of her legs amputated above the knee from diabetes related complications. She was a tough woman, when it was her time to die she went gracefully.

CHAPTER TWELVE

The Roller Coaster of Highs and Lows

"The thief comes only to steal and kill and destroy; I came that they may have life, and have it abundantly."

JOHN 10:10, NASB

Haley Starts School

Although Haley was not quite three, due to her special needs the school allowed her to start attending classes when the Fall school year started.

The classroom was a large room with many stations set up for developmentally challenged individuals. There were about 3 or 4 older students attending plus Haley.

We were introduced to the world of ARDs. ARD is short for Admission, Review, and Dismissal also known as IEP (Individualized Education Program) meetings. The child has to have an existing disability that requires special education and related service needs. Everyone that would be working with Haley was there for the meeting: the principal, teachers, therapists, and a diagnostician. We personally knew everyone and they knew us well. I wasn't intimidated with the process, in fact I liked how thorough they were and I believed they had Haley's best interests in mind. We were blessed to live in a town with such wholesome educators.

They hired a special aid for Haley. It was hard to carry my precious little girl in every day. She was tiny, but absolutely adorable. Everyone loved her and I appreciated that they allowed her to rest when needed. The therapies we had been going out of town for were now being coordinated by the school. The caseworkers who visited our house regularly, now saw her at the school to make sure that she was getting the exercises and services she needed. Our home could be our home again—just us. It was a huge burden lifted off my shoulders. I just didn't know what to do with myself now from 8-3 when Haley was in school.

Nursing School

A neighboring town 16 miles away had a year-long nursing program. Larry and I talked about it and decided that with all the medical training I had gained caring for Haley, nursing school would be a breeze. I had researched every medical terminology the doctors used after every specialist appointment. I felt like I was up for the challenge.

I spent my time wisely while she was in school getting signed up for programs and grants to help with costs. We qualified for a lot of benefits, so it was financially do-able for me to go to school. And since it was a one year program, I just needed someone to care for Haley a couple of hours after school for a short season. "I can do this," I said to myself. It was time to have something to focus on that was bigger than my routine with Haley.

Our friends had just experienced having their baby diagnosed with Down Syndrome. Her mom, Shirley, was coming to live with them to help care for their baby girl. Shirley agreed to pick up Haley from school and care for her each afternoon until I got back in town. That woman was a gift from God. She preferred to be called Nanny, she said that was what her family called her, and that sweet woman certainly became like family to us. Everything fell into place for me to go to nursing school to get my LVN license, and we desperately needed an extra income.

Though I had quit nursing school five years earlier, becoming a nurse this go around was easy. Haley's situation had helped a lot in catapulting me forward. I had compassion and patience mixed with a zeal for learning. I was much more mature and life was as stable as it was going to get. There were two other ladies that I rode with to class every day. We took turns driving and quizzing each other.

I graduated …YES! This girl GRADUATED from nursing school with a 94 overall average. I rocked it! It wasn't easy, but it really was worth it. The only thing I lacked was confidence about taking the licensing test.

I went to Austin, much afraid, and took the state test. It took several days before I knew whether I passed or not—an eternity. When I received the letter in the mail with my LVN license it was truly a triumphant moment.

More Stress

I got a job at our local hospital. I had done some of my clinical training there, and the hospital was only two blocks away from my house. I worked the day shift which was harder, but I needed to be able to pick Haley up from Nanny as soon as I could and spend time with her. With the extra income I was bringing in Larry didn't have to work as many long hours—a blessing.

Great things were happening, but I was beginning to have anxiety attacks and heart palpitations. My stress level was off the charts. I was now responsible for people's lives. If I made a mistake someone might die. I was obsessively diligent. Microbiology had messed me up, and I now had a phobia of germs. A new oddity began of washing my hands so often that they stayed red and ugly.

I endured many sleepless nights, some from worry, others from around the clock care this medically fragile child of ours needed. Haley had breathing issues so a cold was never simple. Winters were hard to get through. She had difficulty swallowing, food was cut up or mashed, but she would choke and aspirate from time to time. Frequent enemas were required to keep her regular and bladder/kidney infections were constant. It wasn't uncommon for her to throw a fit, hold her breath, turn blue, pass out, and automatically start breathing again. It was a physical and emotional roller coaster. There was never any real down time. It was impossible to truly rest and regenerate. The demand was constant.

Communication and Teamwork

A Behavior Specialist came in from the Houston area and sat at our kitchen table discussing ways we could help Haley cope. She couldn't talk, it was frustrating her. We set up a picture symbol system that she would point to that gave us clues to what she wanted. Haley also picked up on simple sign language as a communication tool.

Working full time and caring for Haley was exhausting, hearing her giggles made it all worthwhile. She was a happy baby ... most of the time. My shift at the hospital started at 7:00 a.m. After a sleepless night, that was really early.

We equally shared the care of our daughter. Larry would get up to start the task of getting Haley ready for school and get to work himself by 8:00 a.m. I would bathe her and set out her clothes the night before and a bow to go with it. He was a pro at pony tails, high and tight.

A notebook went back and forth between home and school that we each wrote in to help keep continuity and structure for Haley. Communication was key, between us and the school, we wrote about how she was sleeping, eating, her progress, what distressed her, behaviors, moods, and what needed improving.

Relieving the Stress

Larry and I didn't have a social life. We went to work and came home. Haley was our life. On occasion when I had a weekend off, if we could scrape together gas money and a little spending money we would drive to Oklahoma City. Granny and PawPaw would take care of Haley so we could catch up on much needed sleep and go out to eat or to a movie.

They adored this little bundle of joy. Granny would make chicken and dumplings and banana pudding all from scratch. PawPaw would sit Haley in his lap in his recliner and feed her till her tummy bulged. She was PawPaw's girl even though it was Granny making it happen. No one could soothe her like they could. Wow, did we miss having them live close by.

Anxiety and Fear

Around Christmastime, Larry and I were shopping in a store in Oklahoma City. The store was so crowded that I couldn't find him anywhere. All of the sudden I couldn't breathe, my heart was racing, my legs felt like noodles, and I swore someone was sucking the breath right out of me. That was the first major panic attack I ever experienced, and was only the first of many to come. They happened more and more frequently without notice and seemingly without cause. Waking up with a panic attack wasn't uncommon.

The germ phobia intensified. I was aware of the dangers all around me and felt that if I did anything wrong that God would punish me with an illness or fatal disease. I kept bottles of Germ-X in my car, in my purse, and throughout my house. I became a perfectionist in my behaviors and mannerisms. My home was spotless. As soon as I woke up early in the morning I made the bed. If Larry was still in it, he would have to make up his side when he woke up. I was the only one allowed in my kitchen when I was cooking. My house was so clean you could have eaten off the floor. I wondered if I had missed my calling as a Health Inspector of restaurants. Nah … I would have been far too picky, there wouldn't have been a restaurant allowed to stay open for miles!

Christie wasn't the only one who felt the strain. I felt the stress as well. It was hard shuffling our schedules around with Christie working full time too. We tag teamed as much as we could. It didn't help that Christie's job as a nurse was stressful all on its own. Her anxiety attacks just added another layer to the situation. I hated seeing her panic over things. I wanted to make it all better for her.

Fishing was my stress reliever, but it was hard to go very far from home so I stayed local, pond fishing. Christie and Haley often went with me. We would sit Haley in a chair and give her things to play with. Her favorite toy happened to be my watch until we heard this loud kaploop sound and realized she had gotten tired of it and threw it into the pond. She started giggling because of the sound it made and how the water rippled … could have also been the looks of shock on both of our faces.

Christie's germaphobia did not help matters. One of our biggest fights was when she came home from work on a Saturday earlier than I expected. I had all my fishing lures spread across the kitchen table and my tackle box was going through the dishwasher cycle—it cleaned it really good. Christie freaked when she realized what I was doing.

When Christie started having panic attacks she needed me to be in control when she wasn't. We only relied on each other. Church wasn't a priority, I didn't even know where my Bible was. It was hard to go to church with Haley because she was very noisy. Someone would blow their nose during the service and she'd laugh and have everyone laughing around us which was very disrupting. When she was an infant and toddler age she could go to the nursery, but she was now past that age and too much of a handful to sit in a sanctuary.

Wrong Thinking and Despair

After my mother's death I didn't want to go to church, even though this particular one was special to me. Larry and I said our marriage vows in that sanctuary but I had also seen my mother's dead, lifeless body in there as well. Both were monumental moments.

No one cared if we went to church or not.

I was an adult now, I didn't have to go. My mother's friends attended that church and I felt like they looked at me with pity. "Poor girl, her mother died of cancer and she has that baby with all the problems." I heard their whispers and I hated their stares.

There was no one knocking on our door because they missed seeing us. No one cared if we went to church or not.

There were times when religious fear gripped me because of our decision to pull away from the church. So what if God was mad at me? We both felt that God was punishing us for getting pregnant before being husband and wife. He took our child's mid brain in retribution. We both felt like our sin had caused the birth defect of our innocent daughter. The guilt was more than I could bear. Caring for Haley was overwhelming. I could really have used a church family for support, but that wasn't the situation.

I tried to help Christie with Haley as much as I could. One night Haley started crying in the middle of the night, Christie was sleeping peacefully so I got up as fast as I could to get to Haley before she woke her up. The door to our bedroom was halfway open and I didn't see it in the dark. I hit that door dead centered, right between my eyes at a full run and fell back onto the floor. I was moaning on the floor and Haley was screaming in the other room. Christie jumped out of bed, turned our light on saw me groaning in the floor, said, "Well sh—" as she stepped right over me to care for Haley. I was still laying in the floor groaning when she came back from caring for our daughter. She stepped over me again, turned the light out and went right back to sleep. I finally figured out where I was and what had happened and got back in bed. She had no sympathy for me. At work they asked if I had gotten in a fight, I had two black eyes and my nose was swollen! I was mad. Life was pretty hard.

We can laugh until tears are rolling down our cheeks about those days <u>now</u>, but at the time it was so intense in our household, we weren't laughing much. At times we weren't laughing at all.

Thankfully, we did have periods of relief from stress. There were short increments of time when Haley had no illnesses, our jobs were stable, money was coming in, and we could even invite friends over to play board games or cards. We didn't go out, but felt comfortable with a handful of close friends coming in once in a while.

Finances were much better, and we slowly began to be able to afford to buy new furniture to replace our hand me downs and garage sale treasures. We coasted in between turbulent times. Bills were getting paid ... for now. When times were good, we felt good about things. When times were hard, we felt bad about things. Whatever was happening determined our thinking. When things were difficult we were filled with despair. We didn't hope or trust in God. We made our own way. We did the best we could and felt totally alone.

The Thief

John 10:10 talks about a thief that has come to kill, to steal, and to destroy. The thief that was robbing me was the false idea that I had to have a career in order to BE somebody, and that I needed to help Larry with a second income. Me getting a career actually caused more stress on our little family. We were paying for childcare, I had to have a special insurance because of being a nurse in case of being sued. I required special clothing, and I experienced total exhaustion ... and a whole lot of little things just kept adding up. Working became my scapegoat which put all the burdens on Larry.

Over the years we have clearly seen that our household runs much smoother and with far less stress when I am home taking care of it and Larry is the primary source of income.

God didn't turn His back on us even when we didn't acknowledge He was there. His hand was on us the whole time even when we were filled with wrong thinking and despair. We couldn't see Him, but He was there. We had lost hope, but God knew there were would be a time when leaning on each other wasn't enough. Doing it ALL on our own would exhaust us. He knew that I would hit rock bottom and cry out to Jesus. His precious Son was standing ready to provide all that I needed and so much more.

I wasn't in the flock, but the Shepherd had His eye on me.

I wasn't ready to come to Him yet.

_His precious Son was standing ready
to provide all that I needed and so
much more. I wasn't in the flock, but
the Shepherd had His eye on me._

CHAPTER THIRTEEN

Battle Worn

"You shall see greater things than these."

JOHN 1:50B, NASB

Our Little Miracle

The day we had dreamed of and strived for finally came when our six-year-old precious baby girl, Haley Ann, was at last learning to walk with a walker. Her first doctor told us she would never walk or talk. To our great joy, he was proven wrong. We were determined that Haley would walk, and she did. Countless hours of therapy and dedicated professionals mingled with lots of love and patience taught the rest of her brain to compensate. She could also now say mama, PawPaw, dada, hi, bye, and okay.

Now at 25 years old the toils of life were too much for me to bear, my homemade armor was cracking. Barely coping with what was already on my plate, life hit me hard again. My precious Mom

Melton was dying in a hospital in Abilene, TX. I took a leave of absence from work. Nanny would help Larry with Haley as much as she could. I went and stayed in Abilene, sometimes in her room with her at the hospital and sometimes in a place near the hospital for family. My Auntie Ann, mother's older sister, stayed with Mom Melton too. She was always a comfort to me and I loved her dearly.

Chatting with Auntie Ann was never boring, she was a world traveler. Her husband worked for a gas company that did business throughout the middle east. My cousins had gone to boarding schools in different parts of the world. I loved talking to her and hearing her stories, but I hated the reason we were together.

Losing Mom Melton hit me harder than losing my mother. One morning I was sitting in her room near her bed. She was semi-comatose. On occasion, she would rouse around and talk. She noticed that it was me sitting next to her. She touched my hand and said, "I saw your mother just now, she was so beautiful, picking flowers in Heaven." It meant a lot to me to be there with this precious lady and I loved that she was getting glimpses of Heaven.

She didn't suffer long, it was only a few days later that she joined my mother picking flowers. Mom Melton was surrounded by many of us who loved her dearly when she took her last breath August 24, 1991. I am eternally grateful that I was there.

I drove home after she passed away. It was late at night when I pulled up in our driveway. I immediately noticed one of our newly planted trees broken off. When I walked in the house Larry had a black eye. A friend of his had come over to visit. I'll let Larry tell this one since I wasn't there.

My buddy just stopped by, I didn't see him very often. I had worked with him years ago and knew his family well. He was a few years older than me. We sat in the living room watching an old western movie and talking during the commercials. Haley was asleep in her room. He asked me if I had any liquor to drink, I told him we didn't. We got up and went into the kitchen and I got him a glass of water. He was going through our cabinets and found an old bottle of Tequila that didn't have much in it. He took the bottle and sat down on the couch. While we watched the movie, he finished that bottle off. I noticed he was staring at me, so I looked him eye to eye and asked if he was okay. He said he wanted to go see Haley. I told him that Haley was asleep and we weren't going to bother her. He said, "If I get up and start in there are you going to stop me?"

I said, "Yes, I will."

He looked at me with hard eyes and said, "You're the type of dad that you would do anything to protect her."

"Yes," I replied, my muscles tightened and I was now on my guard.

"If I told you I was going to kill her," he continued, "would you do whatever you could to stop me?"

I stared at him in disbelief, "Why are you talking this way? I think you need to leave."

He got up and started towards the front door, I got up to walk him out. He was at the front door, but turned to go past me towards Haley's room. I grabbed him and forced him out the front door to the yard. He took off running towards the back door and I ran through the house to lock the back door before he got there. Panting, he came back to the front and tried to get into the house once more.

"You are not coming in here," I said loud and clear.

He kept coming towards me, so I grabbed him and took him to the ground in the front yard. Some teenagers with their window down were driving by. I hollered at them to go get the police. When he heard me tell them to get the police, he punched me in the eye. I punched him back in the face several times and told him to get up and leave.

He jumped to his feet in a rage and tore the windshield wipers off his vehicle. Like a wild man he jumped up onto the hood of his car, putting dents in it. My mind raced trying to make sense of what was happening. I was on the alert, there was no way I was going to let him near my house or my daughter.

He jumped off the car and grabbed my tree and broke it off at the ground with his bare hands, He then started towards me again, my goal was to keep him away from my front porch. He tried to get past me to the front door, and I punched him again. The night watchman deputy drove real slow by our house. The out of control, soon to be ex-friend, grabbed me again and we went down to the ground in the front yard. The deputy hollered for me to get away from him as he drove up the street, made a u-turn, then parked in front of my house without getting out of his car.

I had this guy on the ground. Every time he tried to get up I punched him. Sherriff Adams pulled up, and got out of his car. I knew him well and he knew I wasn't a troublemaker. He put his hand on my back and told me to get off of him. I tried to explain that he was out of control and threatening to hurt Haley. He told me he could handle him. Our Sheriff was a big 'ole boy, he was broad shouldered and stood well over 6 feet tall and had years of experience.

Sheriff Adams helped this guy up and asked him what was wrong. In reply, he reared back and punched the Sheriff in the jaw and broke it. It sounded like a shotgun went off when he hit him. Another deputy had showed up and witnessed the punch, got out of his car running, grabbed him, spun him around, and handcuffed him.

I unfriended that guy that day.

A couple of days later I went to the jail and asked him what happened.

"Is Haley okay?" he asked.

"She's fine," I answered. "What the heck was that all about anyway?" I asked him again.

Instead of answering, he asked, "How about you? You okay?"

I shook my head, still trying to figure it all out. "I'm good. I'm fine too."

"You don't have to worry about me coming to your house ever again," he said.

"I think that's a good idea," I responded, still having no clue what his motive was. To this day, I have never seen him again.

Looking back, I don't think he ever intended to hurt Haley, I think he was looking for a fight. He had a lot of life issues going on that had nothing to do with me and he needed a way to relieve his rage. I guess I was his pop off relief valve.

His uncle came by after we returned from Mom Melton's funeral with an expensive gift for Haley. He offered to pay for any damages. I accepted the gift for Haley and told him not to worry about my tree I'd take care of it. I have no ill feelings towards him or his family, God knows I understand what a cruel powderkeg pressure can be.

We didn't choose the battles, they chose us, this incident is a prime example. It was always one battle right on the heels of another with very few periods of rest between.

We didn't choose the battles, they chose us ...

The Funeral

Mom Melton's funeral was simple. At the funeral, an old friend of my mother's that I didn't know told me I reminded her of my mother. I saw family I hadn't seen since my mother's funeral. Afterwards, we went to Mom Melton's trailer house where I had lived with her. Boxes of photos were brought out. We gathered around and went through her cherished memories. My mother's divorce decree was amongst the old photos. My aunt gave me a few photos from her marriage to my biological father, and I took the divorce papers and a couple of dishes.

Losing her really did hit me harder than losing my mother. We had a special relationship and she was my prayer warrior. I didn't stay in contact with her as often as I should have, I knew that God heard her and that she loved me. Knowing that SHE was good enough for Him to love comforted me. I still had stinking thinking. Without her prayers I thought I was doomed.

I wish you could see the smile across my face right now and the humble tears flowing. He changed all of that stinking thinking. Keep reading … my Valiant Warrior King was mounted up, ready to fight my battles for me and be my Prince of Peace.

———————

... just knowing that God heard her and that she loved me. Knowing that she was good enough for Him to love comforted me.

———————

CHAPTER FOURTEEN

Come On In Jesus

———————— ❧ ————————

"Behold, I stand at the door and knock; if anyone hears My voice and opens the door, I will come in to him and will dine with him, and he with Me."

REVELATIONS 3:20, NASB

Love and Morals

Larry grew up with three brothers and two loving parents that taught and lived strong morals and values.

His home was stable.

He went to the same school from second grade through his Senior year of high school.

He had lifelong relationships.

He had his share of whippings, but he'd tell you that he deserved every one of them.

At a young age, him and his older brother, Bobby, had their own lawn mowing business. He was accustomed to hard work and knew that if he wanted nice things, he would have to work hard to get them. His parents taught him and his brothers the love of the Lord in everyday living. He knew love in the church and outside the church. Love was consistent and real to Larry. He didn't carry the emotional baggage that I did, but having Haley had shaken his world as well.

Floating With a Fake Smile

We leaned heavily on each other. When we fought it could get intense, but it was over quickly.

Divorce was not an option.

It took both of us holding each other up and tag-teaming to survive.

To the outside world, it appeared that we were doing just fine.

I imagine that we looked like two ducks gracefully floating on a lake, but beneath the surface we were paddling as hard as we could to keep from drowning in a sea of debt and emotions.

About the time we'd get our finances under control, life would hit us with a huge expense and debt would follow.

I restructured finances for Christie and me with our banker many times.

I remember one time I told him, "You stuck with me when things were good, and I'm going to stick with you now that things are bad." He didn't laugh.

We're proud of ourselves for never having to file bankruptcy.

Every debt I ever owed, I eventually paid off.

Non-Denominational Sounded Good

Larry and I had grown tired of trying to handle everything all on our own. A new church was being built in our small town. it was going to be non-denominational: not Baptist, not Methodist, not Church of Christ, not Pentecostal … we were drawn to it.

The new congregation was made up of about 50 people and they were renting a nearby building that they had remodeled from an abandoned skating rink into a thriving church. The pastor was Rodney Weatherly, a hometown guy. Larry knew him well, he had been his youth leader at the First Baptist Church when he was in high school.

And So, It Began

We began attending. We went to hear a guest speaker and I asked him, "Will our child go to heaven if she were to die?"

He looked at me, wide-eyed and answered, "I don't know."

He was honest at least. He didn't try to give me a platitude or offer theology beyond his depth, but his answer troubled me. I decided that I had to know so I began a research.

We had recently been to see Haley's specialists in Temple, TX, at Scott and White Hospital. She had a new diagnosis of Joubert's Syndrome, and we were told that Haley probably would not live past the age of 25. I had to know if she would go to Heaven and live with Jesus. I had to.

I quizzed Pastor Rodney, he answered, "God is love, He is holy, He is merciful, He is just, and He is gracious." This touched my heart—hearing that God loved my child more than I did, which was more than I could fathom.

In my Baptist background, I had always heard the phrase "the age of accountability," which is basically the belief that God saves everyone who dies before having the ability to make a decision for or against Jesus on their own. In essence, they are automatically saved by God's grace and mercy. There is still much debate on what that age is, and if the age is a number or a capacity for abstract thought and understanding. I knew Haley would not be capable of making a faith decision for or against Jesus, therefore I concluded that the answer was YES, if Haley died she would go to Heaven. This brought me great relief.

We loved going to church with Rodney as the pastor. His sermons made us feel like he had followed us around during the week and had the answers we were seeking to our problems.

He did a whole series on the book of Job, and boy, could we relate.

We attended church every time the doors were opened, not because we feared God's wrath, instead it was because we craved to hear more. We were so hungry for the Word of God, His Bible came alive to us.

We began to build solid friendships with men and women who were so compassionate and nurturing. When we moved into the brand new building it became home to us. We didn't feel judged. We didn't feel like we were an inconvenience, we felt like family.

Greg Smith was the associate pastor. He would carry Haley around the church with him. We adored that man.

I Knew That He Knew

Even though we loved going to church it was still a huge struggle week after week. At times Haley was hard to handle and did not do well sitting still during a service, she would pinch anyone within her reach. We had to sit away from others because this daughter of ours would pull the hair of whoever sat in front of us. We would cringe if someone new came in and sat anywhere near us, those regularly attending knew better.

Even though it was a struggle, we kept coming back.

God was drawing us near to Him, He understood all that we had been dealing with all on our own.

He knew I had stomach ulcers from the countless hours of worrying.

He knew my pain and the abuse I had known as a child.

He knew how alienated from the world we felt.

He saw all the stares we got from people that didn't know what it was like to have a special needs daughter that could only say simple words, screamed out uncontrollably, still wore diapers, had to be carried and spoon fed.

HE KNEW and He was drawing us in under His wing.

Scriptures Came Alive

Psalms 91 became personal, really personal to me. I would meditate on it and put my name in the Psalm.

"Christie who dwells in the shelter of the Most High will abide in the shadow of the Almighty. She will say to the Lord, 'My refuge and my fortress, My God, in whom I trust!' For it is He who delivers Christie from the snare of the trapper and from the deadly pestilence. He will cover her with His pinions, and under His wings Christie may seek refuge; His faithfulness is a shield and bulwark.

Christie will not be afraid of the terror by night, or of the arrow that flies by day; of the pestilence that stalks in darkness, or of the destruction that lays waste at noon. A thousand may fall at her side and ten thousand at her right hand but it shall *not approach Christie. Christie will only look on with her eyes and see the recompense of the wicked.*

I, Christie, have made the Lord, my refuge, even the Most High my dwelling place. No evil will befall me, nor any plague come near my house. For God will give His angels charge over me to guard me in all of my ways. They will bear me up in their hands, that I do not strike my foot against a stone. I will tread upon the lion and cobra. The young lion and the serpent I will trample down.

Because Christie has loved Me, GOD, therefore I will deliver her; I will set her securely on high, because she has known My name. She will call upon Me, and I will answer her; I will be with her in trouble; I will rescue Christie and honor her. With a long life I will satisfy Christie and let her see My salvation."

God meant for us to personalize His Word, this is how scripture came alive to me like it had with Mom Melton and Mrs. D.

I didn't know what every word in scripture meant. Now I know to look up the definitions of the words that stand out to me. For instance, today while writing this, the word bulwark resonated in me so I looked it up. According to Merriam-Webster, a bulwark is something that provides protection for or against something, it is a wall that is built for protection.

Larry and I had begun to pray for a hedge of protection from evil and from harm because we heard others pray that. Now I know that even in our ignorance, He hears us.

"Do not despise these small beginnings, for the Lord rejoices to see the work begin" (Zechariah 4:10, NIV). He really does bless humble beginnings.

Hypocrisy

As a child during the many years of abuse, church was my safe place. I attended 14 schools, kindergarten through 12th grade, so that was probably equivalent to how many churches we became members of also.

Whatever small town we lived in, our family would be active in the local Southern Baptist church. My stepfather would take leadership roles within most of the churches we attended. If the church doors were open, we were there … religiously.

I was taught who God and Jesus were. Holy Spirit was mentioned, but He was basically a stranger. Sort of the silent member of the Trinity.

At the age of 8, I went down the aisle to be saved because my mother prompted me to. I practiced being baptized in the bathtub, but it would be a long time before I actually had to do it, due to the frequent moves.

I had heard preachers say in their sermons that my life would change after I was "saved," but it didn't. I always felt dirty, worthless and insecure, it never changed.

The years I was under my mother and step dad's authority, church to me was just a break from the abuse.

The Real Deal

Country Chapel felt different than any other church I had ever been in. I'm not sure if it was me that was different or the love of the Lord these people freely shared. Whatever it was, it was stirring everything good and bad within me.

Letting Jesus In

The panic attacks and anxiety became worse and more frequent as things I had not dealt with started to surface. I began to relive in my mind all the effects of the abuse I endured as a child, so I asked to talk to Pastor Rodney one on one.

As I sat in his office with tears freely flowing recounting some of what I had been through, he sat across from me behind his desk listening and in deep thought.

Finally he spoke, "The Holy Spirit is telling me that you don't know Jesus as your personal Savior."

I looked up, shocked. "I have been raised in church all my life," I sputtered. "I know who Jesus is." I needed to set the record straight! I was a Baptist girl, even if not a good Baptist girl.

He looked me right in the eyes and said, "Yes, Christie, you know who Jesus is. You know a lot of things about Him, but you don't have a personal relationship with Him. You are living your life all on your own strength."

It was like a dam broke within me, tears flowed like a river. He left the room to get a roll of toilet paper to soak up the grief.

He handed me some tissue and put his hand on my shoulder. "Christie," he said, "Are you ready to ask Jesus to be your Savior? Are you ready to stop shouldering every burden in your life all on your own? Do you want Him to become Lord of your life?"

"YES!" I blurted out, and with my whole heart, I cried out to Him with an audible voice, "Jesus, I need you more than the air I breathe. I need You … I need You …" the tears flowed as He embraced me and I opened my heart to Him.

That moment changed me FOREVER.

Soon after, I was baptized in the horse trough used as a baptistery. (It was a country church after all!)

A Savior, I have a Savior! I am Redeemed!

I thought my heart would burst … a SAVIOR, I have a SAVIOR! I am REDEEMED!

It would take some time for me to really come to know what that fully meant—I am still learning. He keeps revealing Himself to me layer by layer and it is the most fun adventure I have ever known!

I Googled "Savior" one time, curious for a definition. I came across urbandictionary.com. I have no idea who Abbott Brooks is, but he made an entry to Urban Dictionary on January 28, 2004 that defines Savior as: "Jesus Christ. Born in Bethlehem, raised in Nazareth, did miracles in Jerusalem, walked on water, pissed off religious people, was crucified for the sins of the world, went to hell, fought satan, whooped him good, was raised from the dead, sits on a throne, is waiting for his enemies to become his footstool. Holla. Watcha waitin' on. Get saved. You'll still be cool. I'm saved and I'm cool."

I love this definition.

Hope

Everyday life was still challenging, but for the first time ever I didn't feel like Larry and I were alone on this journey. I began to take things one day at a time, looking too far in the future was daunting. I felt love and acceptance … and something new, HOPE.

There was a lot to learn and I had a hunger for knowledge. I had always loved Country music and soft Rock, then a friend at church introduced me to Christian music that spoke to my soul.

I learned that my soul was comprised of my mind, my will, and my emotions and that it was my responsibility to fill it with positive words and ideas. After all those years of stinkin' thinkin' where I let my mind linger in complaint, misery, and despair, it was like a light bulb had been turned on. It was my job to tell my mind what to think, my life didn't get to dictate my thoughts.

At church, Larry and I soaked in every word taught. The study on the book of Job in the Bible continued to resonate in me. We could certainly relate to Job's calamity. I began to ponder our own trials and tribulations, asking God about why He allowed them.

In my mind, I began to picture a conversation between God and Satan about Larry and me. In this conversation, God was looking down from Heaven at us while we were dating and falling in love. He was pleased that we were making good choices by not doing drugs and even though we had both drunk alcohol on occasion with friends, it was rare. We weren't troublemakers. His smile was upon us. Satan commented that I didn't belong to Jesus, he had plans of his own for me. Satan was reminding God that I was pregnant and unmarried. He told God that these two teenagers they were looking upon weren't blameless. "They have sinned against You, God."

God kept smiling and told Satan, "I will allow you to do as you will, but there will be a day when Christie will stand tall against you as a Mighty Warrior, glorifying Jesus throughout the world."

Satan laughed, "I see no potential."

I am so glad that God saw my potential, He created it.

In my vision after Satan left the scene I had my own conversation with God, "Why did You allow our child to be born with so many health issues and with part of her brain missing? We went through countless genetic testings, we were the first in our families to go through this. Haley's diagnosis is Joubert Syndrome, Agenesis of the Corpus Callosum, and Microcephaly. Geneticist give us a 25% chance of it happening again because of the unknown, they even referred to it once as possibly environmentally related. Why? I have been told it happens to 1 in 4,000 ... whether those statistics are valid or not, I don't know ... but You do. What I do know is that what has happened to our Haley is EXTREMELY rare!"

I have no doubt He knew all the stats and information I quoted Him, but I felt bold and comfortable in asking God Almighty, the Creator of the Universe, Abba Father "WHY US?"

He was gentle and kind with me, He knew my heart was not against Him. He said, "You live in a fallen world, the enemy goes around seeking out who he can destroy. I knew that by yourselves, you and Larry would have continued in feeling utterly hopeless. I had a plan for you, and every human on the Earth. I sent Jesus, My beloved Son to be your Savior and Holy Spirit to be your Comforter. I knew that when you chose My Son to be Lord of your home that no calamity could overtake you. You are overcomers in Jesus."

I still didn't completely understand why Larry and I had been given such a big portion of trials and tribulations, but I was fully comforted in knowing that HE was fully aware of all that was happening. I didn't feel judgment and I was no longer angry with Him. God knew that this would not crush me, this would create strength in me. He knew I was a vessel of noble use.

He spoke to me, *"... **Does not the potter have the right over the clay, to make from the same lump one <u>vessel for honorable use</u> and another for common use"*** (Romans 9:21, NASB). He knew I was no ordinary woman, He had created me to be extraordinary.

Like King David I petitioned my Potter to:

"Create in me a clean heart, O God, and renew a steadfast spirit within me. Do not cast me away from Your presence and do not take Your Holy Spirit from me. Restore to me the joy of Your salvation and sustain me with a willing spirit. Then I will teach transgressors Your ways, and sinners will be converted to You."

PSALM 51:10-13, NASB

Prayers are just a fancy name for conversations with God.

CHAPTER FIFTEEN

The Blessing

> The hand of God was also on Judah to give them one heart to do what the king and the princes commanded by the word of the Lord.
>
> 2 CHRONICLES 30:12, NASB

Foster Parenting

We tried to provide foster care for children who were abused and neglected for a couple of years.

Larry and I both felt like it was too big of a risk to have any more biological children of our own. With our stress level and the constant care Haley required, we just didn't feel we could risk it.

We had the privilege of caring for several kiddos for different lengths of time.

One little boy was very dear to us. I wish it could have worked out for us to have adopted him, but we had more than we could handle and had to give up foster care parenting. It was best for all of us. This dear little boy was adopted a couple of years later by a couple who had no children, that comforted us in knowing we had done the right thing.

Foster parenting put us in all kinds of situations. For instance, I became an expert in handling lice. We lived not far from I-40, known as the drug trafficking corridor. Late one night we got a phone call from our caseworker that two children needed emergency placement overnight. Their caregivers had been incarcerated for trafficking a large amount of drugs.

Larry took the boy, I took the young girl, both were under the age of five. They were in desperate need of a bath. We went to separate bathrooms.

The caseworker left us some clean clothes and a few supplies before she walked out the door. They had nothing of their own.

The young girl had thick, dark hair that hadn't been washed in a while. As I was gently scrubbing her head and lathering her up with lots of bubbles I noticed little tiny bugs. I stayed calm, never freaked out, just kept talking to her as she played in the bubbles. I rinsed her off really good. The whole time I was in deep thought, wondering what I was going to do. I wasn't prepared for this. I didn't have any lice killer. I decided that I would use Larry's comb on her hair, it would be cheaper to replace. We would make a pallet on the floor for them with blankets and pillows I could throw into hot water and a hot dryer. They would only be with us overnight. I was to drive them to Amarillo the next morning.

As I was combing through her hair the lice were so thick that I had to rinse the comb out and wash them down the sink.

She never knew I was totally freaking out on the inside.

Larry was dealing with basically the same scenario in the other room. I could tell as soon as I saw his face when we met in the living room.

Christie's 101 on Getting Rid of Lice

This was my very first time to deal with lice.

I hate to admit that I became an expert, but nevertheless, I became much more prepared after that and now I have the safest method of getting rid of those critters.

Mayonnaise ... people! I don't like to use chemicals, especially on kiddos, so I did lots of research. To get rid of lice, start with dry hair and apply lots of mayonnaise, comb it through, then put a disposable shower cap on. Place the kid in a tub of warm water with toys, let them play for 30 minutes to an hour.

If it was a bad case, I did it for as long as the kid would tolerate it.

Next you wash their hair with Dawn liquid dishwashing soap once, then wash it again with your regular shampoo. Use a Nit comb, which is a fine-tooth comb, and start at the crown of their head and work down, strand by strand to get all the eggs off. I would repeat this process if I felt like they needed it.

It worked every time! It's also very nourishing to the hair.

During our foster care season, I kept lots of mayo on hand in the pantry for lice emergencies!

Specialized Pediatric Nurse

I felt restless working at the hospital. I wanted a new adventure.

I got a job working as a home health nurse caring for other children that were more medically fragile than Haley. These pediatric patients had tracheostomies and gastrostomy tubes. Caring for kids worse off than my Haley helped me keep our own struggles in perspective.

I was gone long hours, traveling all over the panhandle of Texas.

I had a portable bag phone I kept with me. That was the first cell phone I had ever used, and it was incredible technology at the time.

Nanny helped us with Haley. Larry picked her up at 5:00 p.m. each day after he got off.

His job responsibilities had been changing. He drove the propane truck part of the time and the rest of the time he did the paperwork and took on the office responsibilities. He had gotten a promotion and a raise.

The Blessing | 141

Being a Pediatric Home Health Nurse required too much time away from home and in the end was not worth the money. I kept up the pace for a couple of years, then gave my notice and started working as a private duty nurse.

Freely Making a Difference

I cared for the child of a doctor who was temporarily living in a neighboring town 16 miles from home. She had Spina Bifida.

Spending time with this child's mom allowed me to connect to my own heart and soul. She awakened ideas in me. Brainstorming with her was fun.

We made a great team with another mom of a child with Down's Syndrome. Together we created a nonprofit organization in our area to help other families with children with special needs. It was a great support group that brought about community awareness.

Countless hours were volunteered and a passion for helping in the community began to take root in both Larry and me.

Ask and It Shall Be Given …

We both began to desire more in life, we wanted financial freedom … and another child.

Fear of what happened to Haley happening again with another child began to surface, but we trusted God that if it was meant for us to have more children He would bless our prayers.

We specifically prayed that I would get pregnant if it was His will. If it wasn't His will, we prayed for Him to NOT let it happen!

It happened immediately.

I triple checked it with two home pregnancy tests and a doctor visit. We were both excited and concerned at the same time.

I was thirty years old, Larry thirty-two, Haley ten.

My Encounter

GOD KNEW. He had an encounter planned. I had been on a waiting list and was scheduled to go on the Walk to Emmaus, a Christian retreat, the week after I found out I was pregnant. So, at 7 weeks pregnant with my second child, I went.

My sponsor for the retreat was Pastor Rodney's wife, Debra. Months of prayer and preparation went into this retreat. Debra had people writing letters and sending cards to be given to me at the appointed time.

There were groups of people praying for me during this three-day encounter with the Creator of the Universe, Yahweh. Some I knew, some I didn't, but they joined the host of Heaven and made intercession for me.

I had no idea what God had planned.

I had no concept of time. Watches and clocks of every nature were removed.

For three days, the outside world was shut out and I was saturated with agape love and learning more about what it meant to have Jesus as my Savior.

It was Heaven on Earth behind those closed doors.

On the second night, I woke up to music playing in the background, it was beautiful. I wanted to know where it was coming from.

The world outside my window was dark, I had no idea what time it was, my roommate was sound asleep.

I opened the door to look in the hallway, I could still hear the music playing and was curious as to where it was coming from.

As I walked down the lit hallway I followed the sound to the door of the sanctuary. When I opened the door, there wasn't a soul in there. No one.

I stopped hearing the music when I entered into the sanctuary. Perplexed, I sat down. I decided that since I was wide awake anyway and no one else was around I deeply wanted to talk to God … so I did.

I poured out my fears and concerns about this baby, the "what ifs" began spewing from what had been trapped within me.

I sat and sobbed with my hands covering my face.

I told the Lord of Creation that I didn't think I could handle it if He allowed this child to have birth defects too.

"What if it was me that was defective?" I worried, "What if I carried a gene that wasn't compatible with Larry's genes?"

I sat there only minutes, but it was 10 years of painful thoughts, fears, and insecurities that were released to the only ONE who had the answers.

He allowed me to say it all, and I did it with great respect, never blaspheming Him. I just poured out my heart to Him. I poured out my pain—raw and unpolished, real and unrestrained.

When I finished, He spoke directly to my soul. It wasn't an audible voice that someone tangibly sitting beside me could have heard, but I heard Him clearly, inside me, deep in my knower.

"I have gotten you through everything in the past, I never left your side. I have given you strength to get through every situation, I will not ever leave you."

Peace like I had never felt before came over me.

Peace like I had never felt before came over me.

Even though He didn't say this child would be born "normal," there it was, deep in my knower that all was well.

In that sanctuary, I began singing and praising Him.

My voice sounded like a choir of angels, the acoustics were good.

As I sang I felt like there wasn't anything that the enemy could throw at me that I couldn't get through with God's help.

He had delivered me from utter despair and was preparing me for my destiny.

My Covenant Promise

I promised the Lord that I would raise this child, boy or girl, to serve Him and I knew when I made this promise that it was a covenant between the GREAT I AM and me. God sealed the covenant with His bountiful love and treasured this mother's heart. I knew He would give me the wisdom and heart needed to raise such a child.

Pregnancy

The pregnancy wasn't easy, fear of what could go wrong lived very close to the surface. There were many ultrasounds to make sure the brain was fully forming and blood tests checking for abnormalities, none were found.

Contractions started way too early in the pregnancy so bed rest was required.

I had been working as a nurse for a home health agency since my private duty nursing for the doctor had stopped. Reluctantly, I took a leave of absence.

A teenage girl in our church volunteered to come live with us for the summer to help with Haley. Sara was a delight and a blessing. She was so good with Haley. I couldn't have special ordered a more fitting helper. I felt God's blessings. She stayed in the baby's room.

We had beautifully decorated the nursery in rich jewel tones. The baby bed was a brass bed we borrowed and we bought a brass cradle to match it. The babies bedding had paisley print all over it. We matched wall paper to go with the bedding. It was a very rich and classy room with teddy bears. A twin-size bed was set up in the corner for Sara.

Sara had signed up to go on a mission trip long before she came to stay with us. The trip was three weeks before my due date and she was to be gone only a week so we weren't overly worried. With our blessings, she went on the mission trip.

It's Time

The baby decided to come three weeks early. Sara hadn't even been gone two days. In the middle of the night, in my sleep, my water broke. It was a LOT of water. I remember rolling over and feeling like I was in a bathtub. I woke Larry up before the tidal wave hit him and drenched him.

He jumped up and called Granny and PawPaw since they needed at least three hours' notice to drive in from Oklahoma City to care for Haley. Until they could arrive, his brother and sister-in-law, Ronny and Sherri agreed to care for her.

It was a 2-hour drive to the hospital in Amarillo. I wanted to take my time and not have to be in the hospital waiting. On the way, I casually suggested going to the 24-hour Wal-Mart to walk around till the contractions were stronger. Larry almost lost it and exclaimed rather loudly, "NO!" He was the level headed one and quickly told me I was going directly to the hospital. He was not going to argue about it.

When we arrived at 4:00 am we entered through the ER. They quickly placed me on a gurney since it had been 3 hours from the time my water broke.

He told the nurses that I had insisted on cleaning everything before we left since my mother-in-law would be coming to stay. They completely understood. What woman wouldn't?

I didn't like elevators so I hopped off the gurney and told the nurses I would meet them upstairs and walk the stairs. Once again I was trumped ... unanimously!

Defeated, I got back on the gurney and a nurse began to wheel me into the elevator. The lights were strobing on and off inside, I put one foot on each side of the doors to stop the gurney and told them no way was I going in THAT elevator.

The one next to it opened up brightly lit, I went in and went up.

You're just going to have to find out the rest of the story in the next book *Beauty in the Storm ...*

Watch for Beauty in the Storm ...

E P I L O G U E

Thank you for going with me on this journey of discovery as God revealed to me my identity as a vessel of noble use for Him. Prior to my encounter with Jesus in Pastor Rodney's office at the age of 26, I felt no value as a human being. When I stepped into true relationship with Jesus, I came to know Him as my Redeemer. Because of Jesus I became a new creation just like the Apostle Paul talked about:

Therefore if anyone is in Christ, he is a new creature; the old things passed away; behold, new things have come.

2 CORINTHIANS 5:17 NASB

To be honest, it took me YEARS to truly understand the GRACE this verse was saturated with because so much religiosity had been engrained in me. Papa God, Jesus, and Holy Spirit have lovingly taught me to think differently. I am here to tell you that the journey is worth it.

When you return with me and begin reading the second book in the Monumental Moments series, *Beauty In The Storm*, you will see how Jesus helped us clean up some messes that weren't of our doing. The storms of life took us by surprise. On occasion we could see them brewing in the distance, but most of them came without warning.

During one of my fiercest storms, Jesus was there with me. I honestly wanted to be swallowed up by the waves of grief that daily overpowered me. My darkest days were spent in deep mourning. Larry and I grieved differently, which pushed us apart. This storm was meant to destroy our faith and our marriage. We felt betrayed by God and we wanted NOTHING to do with Him. We left the church.

God showed off His MAGNIFICENCE and He wasn't offended when I told Him I wanted NOTHING to do with Him. Oh … and I didn't get struck by lightening because I was angry at God!

Jesus NEVER left my side. At my tipping point, He showed me a vision of being held and Him crying with me. That kind of LOVE is what brought me out of the darkness. He was there to administer healing and restoration.

I learned some valuable life lessons in that particular storm. Holy Spirit kept me alive this side of Heaven … find out how in *Beauty in The Storm*.

APPENDIX

The Story of the Cover Painting

By Victoria Peterson, Artist

"I've been trying so hard and I'm done. I can't do it anymore." I remember crying, no actually sobbing to God one day. Ten years ago I had begun my "career" as a prophetic or some would say worship artist with painting my very first painting on stage at a conference featuring Morningstar's Rick Joyner and White Dove Ministries' Paul Keith Davis at my home church in Wasilla Alaska. It had just been me pouring my heart out to Jesus with a very child-like painting of some waves and the sun breaking through the clouds. Little did I know that night was my debut as one of a very few prophetic artists in Alaska who would go on to be invited to paint at just about every conference in my area with two other artists for the next year and a half, ministering as "Art is Worship."

At the same time, I began teaching kids art classes in a studio that I opened, called Doodles. I had spent the past 10 years working and ministering as an artist. I could write my own book of all the trials, hurts, success, and lessons learned along the way and Jesus answered my cry that day that I told him I was done, "You're done? Good. Now I can step in." I can hear that answer now as I write this.

An opportunity presented itself in the form of a book launch for a favorite couple of mine, the Bethkes. They had a book coming out and I decided to apply to be on their team. I needed something in my life that was purely for pleasure, and I really wanted to support other Christian artists that I believed in; be a part of their ministry. Following their ministry was a part of my season when I lost my twin daughters in my second trimester of pregnancy. It was so much fun launching their book! It got me thinking that maybe, just maybe I could illustrate one day. I had always toyed with the idea of illustrating and my mom and one of my many sisters talked about writing children's books. I was allowing myself to dream a great big God dream. I decided to ask the Launch Team leader, Anna Lebarron, for advice on where to start. One thing led to another and Anna hired me to create two logos for her. She needed a graphic artist, but I decided that I would draw her up something anyways to see if I could make her vision come to life. I think I did, and I was stoked to have done a good job for such a fabulous person.

I received a message one morning when I opened my social media "Hi Victoria, I'm a writer with a book coming out ... could you draw me an original peacock that has my character ... your drawings are beautiful."

I think I may have called all my family members, ran around the house, laughed, and even cried! "Thank you, Jesus!"

She invited me to browse her profile and blog. Christie Jones radiated joy. Right away, she reminded me of a fellow artist friend that I first met in my first year of prophetic art ministry named Joy Lynn. I didn't know why. Maybe it was the joy I felt through her writing?

Our first conversation via phone ended with my most dreaded subject: money. Breaking the mold of professionalism, I opened up to my new author friend about how awkward it is to talk money with my clients. I mean, my gift had been introduced to the world in a church as I worshiped God. It felt weird to be doing what I was called to do and ask for money. So she asked me to ask God for a number if I felt comfortable doing it. I was so relieved and encouraged that this was the caliber of person that I was working with. What a relief. "Yes, let's ask God!"

Right away I felt he answered. I called my mom up and asked her to pray for a number and without hesitation she confirmed what I was feeling. The exact word. Eeeeek!!! I was so stoked that He cared and delivered an answer right away!

The process of developing Christie's character began. She wanted a peacock to represent her brand. She loved the idea of a regal peacock that resembled her. Several drawings later and feedback back and forth between us, I had a completed peacock with a smile. She wore a crown and was in full strut—Christie as a regal cartoonish peacock. Done. Not satisfying, but job done and I had hoped my client got what she desired. And then she asked me a question that changed it all. "Do you feel that this drawing was Holy Spirit inspired?" To that I had a very long answer. I told her a story of the last project (a memorial portrait) I had worked on that just felt wrong UNTIL I let the Holy Spirit lead me. I told myself that I wouldn't do any other commissions without the freedom of being led by Him. I had gotten caught up in doing exactly what was envisioned for Christie's character that I pushed back what I had been feeling, which was Christie with white feathers in her dress. Christie wearing a crown. Beautiful characteristics of a peacock, but Christie. God wanted her, not a cartoon version of her. As I began to paint, I saw her standing on top of a mountain looking at an expanse of mountain peaks, clouds blanketing below. No valleys, just peaks.

Two days after I began the painting that Holy Spirit was leading, I received a word from my dear artist friend. The same friend that unexplainably reminded me of Christie when I first started reading about her. It was Joy Lynn. She had had a dream and received a word from the lord concerning me after praying for me through her ministry that she calls, Love Letters From Abba.

"As soon as I prayed for you and fell asleep I began to see something, which I can only describe as seeing through your eyes. Abba shows me things with people I know and trust but through your eyes as if I am seeing a piece of your life transpire with my own people surrounding me, so that I will understand how to interpret ... I saw you on the top of this mountain and there were snow covered mountain peaks as far as I could see. In the far distance I could see and hear a bald eagle flying towards you. It flew closer and closer gliding and circling on the air currents. It took its time and patiently continued its pattern of floating down in air current circles and only expending energy to rise in order to once again rest and flow while moving nearer and nearer towards you. I then saw the sunrise at the furthest peak which brought light across the entire expanse of those peaks. The interesting part is I didn't see any valleys. Usually when you see an eagle it will be flying through a valley in order to see. But, this eagle was purposefully flying high above the mountain peaks ..."

My friend was seeing me on the mountain peak. I was seeing and painting Christie on that peak. The process of painting became a huge spiritual battle as all hell broke loose in my home. Several family members near death, admitted into the hospital. Financial struggles like we had never seen. Attacks on my children. A friend's death. An assault on my daughter and her friend that ended in the person being arrested. I had to believe that something huge was breaking in the spiritual realm for the attack to be so severe. It was like every single day was a fight to get the painting done. Most of those moments painting were deep into the night with worship music playing through headphones, sometimes nursing my baby, barely awake. It was warfare.

"This is how I fight my battles, it may look like I'm surrounded but I'm surrounded by You ... " ... a line from a song that another friend sent me in the midst of the process. I fought the battles surrounding

my first Holy Spirit-inspired book cover through worship. And sometimes worship looks a lot like raising a family and nursing a baby in my pajamas half asleep while painting what He sees. I'm so thankful that my journey took me to a place where I was done trying and He took over.

The result is the painting on the cover of this book, *Vessel of Noble Use*. It is the beginning of a new chapter for me ...

Victoria Peterson, Artist
www.northerngypsies.com
Instagram: CANVASCAFEALASKA

9 781732 100800